Viburnum

Lloyd Kenyon

NCCPG National Plant Collection Holder

Photographs by the author

This publication has been funded by
the author

ISBN: 0-9533875-6-9

Published by
The National Council for the Conservation
of Plants and Gardens (NCCPG)
Stable Courtyard
Wisley Garden
Woking
Surrey
GU23 6QP

Printed by
Evonprint, Small Dole, West Sussex BN5 9XE Telephone: 01273 494631

CONTENTS

FOREWORD

I started collecting *Viburnum,* rather slowly at first, in 1992, having been captivated by the wonderful early summer scent of *Viburnum* x *juddii* growing close to the house. By 1998, having collected more than 100 viburnums I was granted provisional National Plant Collection® status which was followed in 2000 with the grant of full National Plant Collection® status. There are now well over 200 viburnums in the collection most of which are mentioned in the following pages, these are shown ❀. As I do not publicly express any favourites I have not included any obvious indicators as to which I consider best for particular situations, but I hope that there are sufficient guiding hints throughout the text.

Amongst these hints are the Award of Garden Merit (AGM) given by the Royal Horticultural Society. These awards have been granted in various forms since before 1860 but were reviewed in 1984 and again in 1993 to remove some of the older cultivars from the list. Although awards prior to 1993 are technically invalid, for the sake of completeness I have included all awards, those that were confirmed at the time of the review are shown as 1993 but have the original date preceding in brackets e.g. AGM (1960)1993. Those that were not confirmed merely have the original date in brackets. There have been no new awards to viburnums since the 1993 review.

When I first started collecting *Viburnum* I soon discovered that there was no definitive work on the genus. A telephone call to the Librarian at the RHS Lindley Library not only confirmed this, but he made the helpful suggestion to 'trawl the literature'. Over the past three years I have trawled, mainly in the RHS Lindley Library and the library at the Royal Botanic Gardens, Kew, and more recently on the Internet. The Bibliography (p. 83) is a small selection of the more important sources that have contributed to the information in this book.

As a result of continuing study, the Floras of the world are constantly being revised and I am aware of one significant omission from the Bibliography, namely the recently published *Flora of China*, which I have not been able to study in time to include. In particular this has highlighted the confusion between *V. awabuki* and *V. odoratissimum* which is succinctly explained by Roy Lancaster in his article *Viburnum Conundrum* (*The Garden* November 2000).

In treading the tortuous path of addressing the genus *Viburnum* I know that I will stand guilty in some eyes of errors, omissions and unsubstantiated alterations for which I should perhaps apologize, but as an amateur I bow to those whose years of professional training and experience allows them bolder statements than I would dare to make. Unless I have specifically stated that an opinion is my own, the information has been gleaned from those works listed in the Bibliography or others.

Lloyd Kenyon

INTRODUCTION

In what other genus can you find such diversity of characteristics: evergreen or deciduous, fragrance, beauty and size of flowers, interesting leaf textures, a variety of sizes to suit every garden, spectacular autumn colours and conspicuous berries, many of which hang on the bare branches well into winter when they take on a translucent appearance after the first frosts? It is no exaggeration to say that with a handful of judiciously chosen viburnums, they can be in flower for much of the year, and even when they are not, their other attractions make them essential as part of any garden, however small. Viburnums are tolerant of a wide range of soil conditions, present few difficulties in cultivation, and suffer only rarely from diseases or pests.

Viburnum species are widely distributed across the world, predominately in the northern hemispheres of both east and west; although there are some 250 species in all, only four, *V. lantana, V. opulus, V. rigidum* and *V. tinus* are natives of Europe and North Africa. Some 20 species are natives of North America, and another 60 or so come from Central and South America, but more than half of the known species come from Asia, where new species continue to be found. Unfortunately most nurserymen and landscape architects have confined their attentions to a bare dozen or so of the species, relying on the variety of the well-known crosses and cultivars, and sadly neglecting the less common ones; many are now lost to cultivation.

With only two native species in the British Isles, *Viburnum lantana* and *Viburnum opulus*, which, whilst having some noteworthy aspects, generally lack the more exotic attributes, our gardens would have been very much the poorer if it had not been for the wealth of horticultural exploration at the end of the nineteenth and the first half of the twentieth century, which has made so many plants available to gardeners today. Added to this is the large number of hybrids that have been raised by those enthusiasts whose aim is to intensify the specific qualities of the original species. The result is that today there are more than 150 different viburnums available to the gardener, as currently listed in *The RHS Plant Finder*.

No introduction to a book on viburnums would be complete without an acknowledgement of the work done by Dr. Donald Egolf at the United States National Arboretum; a brief glance at the list of his works in the Bibliography will confirm his contribution. After writing his dissertation on viburnums at the Pennsylvania State University he took up a Fulbright scholarship at the University of London, and studied at the John Innes Horticultural Institute and the Royal Botanic Garden, Edinburgh, before returning to the United States. Here he commenced his work as a research horticulturist at the National

Arboretum, taking with him much of the Cornell collection on which his dissertation had been based. Between 1966 and 1988 he released a total of eighteen cultivars and hybrids, all of which carry American Indian names, before tragically losing his life in a car accident.

DESCRIPTION OF VIBURNUMS

Erect or sprawling shrubs or small trees belonging to *Caprifoliacae*. The leaves opposite, simple, deciduous or evergreen, stipulate or estipulate, petiolate, entire or serrate-dentate or trifid, pinnately or palmately veined. The flowers in cymose corymbs, actinomorphic, hermaphrodite, but sometimes the marginal flowers of the inflorescence are enlarged, somewhat zygomorphic and sterile. Calyx 5-lobed. Corolla white, creamy or pink, 5-lobed, rotate, campanulate, hypocrateriform or tubular, imbricate in bud. Stamens five, adnate to the corolla, alternate with the corolla lobes. Anthers dorsifix, versatile, longitudinally dehiscent. Style short, conical; stigma 3-lobed, sessile. Ovary inferior, 3-celled, one of the cells containing a single suspended ovule, the others abortive. The fruit a drupe crowned by the persistent calyx and style, with a single globose pyrene. Endocarp horny or stony, often undulate in cross-section or with inflexed edges; albumen often ruminate.

Ray Flowers

A feature of some of the *Viburnum* species is the mixture of both fertile and sterile flowers arranged in what is often referred to as a Queen Anne's lace pattern, a characteristic that they share with the lacecap hydrangeas. The numerous fertile flowers are arranged at the centre of the inflorescence surrounded by an outer row or rows of sterile flowers. The fertile flowers are small, generally up to 5mm in diameter and are quite insignificant compared to the much larger sterile flowers which can be up to 50mm in diameter. Undoubtedly the purpose of the sterile flowers is to attract pollinating insects which then visit the fertile flowers.

A curious aspect of the ray flowers is their variability of symmetry, the petals on the outer side of the inflorescence often being considerably larger than those facing the centre. This is most marked in *V. plicatum*, and to a lesser extent in *V. furcatum* and *V. lantanoides*, whilst in *V. opulus* the ray flowers are almost entirely symmetrical.

Hardiness

It follows from the diversity of climatic conditions in the regions where viburnums are found, that there is an equally wide range of hardiness; whilst those from the higher regions of the Himalaya and the northern United States can be expected to put up with anything the British climate can produce, those from sub-tropical or tropical zones would only survive in the mildest areas, and, even then, would probably not thrive.

Perhaps the biggest problem that they have to encounter is the unpredictability of the British climate. Warm early springs in February and March will encourage the buds to burst and the leaves to develop, only to encounter a cold snap in April; even if the frost does not damage the tips, the weight of a fall of snow can break the well-leaved branches and destroy the shape of the plant for years to come. For this reason the US Hardiness Zones which are attributed to many of the species should be treated with a degree of caution.

In 1998, after an unseasonably warm March, there was just such a weather pattern; a mild frost was followed by a fall of 15-20cm of damp, heavy snow which blanketed the young plants, bending to the ground those branches that it did not break. The only casualties observed on the North Wales/Shropshire border were:

Slight frost damage to leaves of *V. cinnamomifolium, V.* x *hillieri, V. japonicum, V. odoratissimum, V. odoratissimum* 'Emerald Lustre', *V. plicatum* 'Nanum Semperflorens' and *V.* x 'Pragense'.

Severe frost damage to leaves and growing tips of *V. atrocyaneum, V. betulifolium, V. cylindricum, V.* x *hillieri* 'Winton'.

V. erubescens also showed severe damage to leaves and growing tips, but the hardier *V. erubescens* var. *gracilipes* was unaffected, some degree of redress by confirming that the plants were correctly named in the first place!

Propagation

Many viburnums are suckering shrubs which makes their propagation by division one of the simplest methods. Some are also inclined to layer themselves (see *V. lantanoides*) which again provides a simple means of increasing the stock.

The more usual means of propagation by cuttings is generally most successful, for the deciduous species; softwood cuttings taken in June or July will root within four weeks in a mist propagator with a bottom heat of 20°C. For the evergreen species semi-hardwood cuttings taken in August or September are better, rooting within two months with the same bottom heat.

Grafting of selected cultivars is often practised, particularly of *V. carlesii* and related hybrids which can be slow to root as cuttings, but should be exercised with care, as all too often the competition between the graft and the rootstock results in the rootstock taking over.

Viburnums can also be grown from seed which should be sown immediately it is ripe in trays in a cold frame protected from mice and birds. If the trays are brought into a warm greenhouse in March germination may take place more quickly. However germination may take more than a year, particularly with the autumn fruiting varieties, as a warm period followed by a cold period is required to initiate germination. As viburnums are both self-fertile and self-compatible (within their respective Section, see page 13), there remains the danger when growing from seed that hybrids will be produced or that poor quality pollination will lead to inferior plants.

Fruiting

Apart from the sterile viburnums which, whilst acknowledged as the most attractive of garden plants with their large rounded flower trusses, are biological freaks, the genus as a whole shows a reluctance to self-pollinate. They will always give a more reliable display of fruit if there has been pollination from another species or a nearby plant of the same species (preferably from a different clone). The case of *V. davidii* is interesting, where for a long time it was held that the plant was dioecious, that is, having male flowers on one plant and female flowers on another. While 'male' and 'female' plants are still sold separately by some nurserymen, it is much more likely that this is nothing more than a greater emphasis being placed on the rejection of self-pollination than the anomalous sexual behaviour of one species out of the whole genus.

Pruning

Most viburnums do not require pruning except when it is necessary to keep the larger forms in shape in a smaller garden. Indeed pruning *V. plicatum* and its cultivars will destroy its unique horizontal habit which, when well grown, gives it its characteristic pyramid-shaped structure and its outstanding appearance when covered in bloom. If pruning is necessary, it is best carried out after flowering or during the dormant period.

The evergreen *Viburnum* species in particular will produce a greater numbers of flower buds if the terminal buds are pinched out to promote branching. If this is to be carried out successfully it should be done before mid-July as many of the species set flower buds in the late summer and autumn.

Cultivation

When it comes to cultural conditions viburnums are one of the least fussy of shrubs. The soil should be reasonably free draining but most will tolerate diverse soil conditions although a slightly acid soil with a pH between 6.0 and 6.5 is preferable. The Asiatic species are said to be more tolerant of calcareous soils than their American counterparts. The exceptions to this are *V. acerifolium, V. furcatum* and *V. lantanoides* which will thrive in a more acid soil with a pH as low as 4.5 to 5.0.

The majority can be grown in full sun, indeed it is essential for those which are expected to give a good display of autumn colour, but the variegated and yellow-leaved forms will give a better display if they are grown in partial shade and *V. furcatum* and *V. lantanoides* suffer scorched leaves if they are not grown in shade.

Pests and Diseases

Viburnums do not suffer greatly from pests, the most common being aphids which attack particularly *V. opulus* although *V. trilobum*, which is physically almost indistinguishable, does not appear to be so seriously affected. The usual army of thrips and scale insects will be found, but they do not do any harm. The only serious pest, which is most severe in the Section Opulus, is the viburnum leaf beetle *Pyrrhalta viburni* a winged, though reluctant flyer which, together with its larvae, feeds on the leaves leaving a skeleton of veins. This can be controlled by chemical means, alternatively the affected branches should be cut out and burned between early autumn and late spring when the eggs have been laid in pits in the stems of the young twigs. *Viburnum tinus* is said to be susceptible to viburnum white fly which was first recorded in Britain in 1944 but does not appear to be widespread.

Likewise the usual list of diseases can be found in viburnums though none have any lasting effect provided that the necessary precautions are taken against them; as with so many shrubs the simple precaution of raking up fallen leaves to deny the fungus a safe haven for the winter will pay dividends the following spring. *Viburnum plicatum* in particular is prone to wilt, often brought about by drought stress, caused by botryosphaeria canker which causes the branches to die back, the only solution being to remove and burn the infected branches as quickly as possible to remove the fruiting fungus which appears as pin-head

11

sized black pimples along the branch. Downy and powdery mildews are also encountered but their damage is limited and are usually a result of unfavourable climatic conditions. Bacterial leaf spot causes round, water-soaked spots about 3-4mm in diameter on the leaves and young stems but is rarely severe enough to disfigure more than a few leaves; if the infestation is excessive a Bordeaux mixture will control it.

Nomenclature

The well-known problems of nomenclature are found in the genus *Viburnum* as they are in most other genera, but the Science and Horticultural Advice Committee of the Royal Horticultural Society is regularly addressing them. However, just as Rome was not built in a day, so the Committee cannot wave a magic wand to eradicate all the invalid names, both cultivars and species, that have been coined by nurserymen over the years. Many of the synonyms, particularly where there has been a significant change in the name (e.g. from *V. fragrans* to *V. farreri*), are well documented and, in some cases, discussed in the text, but the simpler orthographic variations have been largely ignored as there is no limit to the number of errors that a nurseryman can make when writing a label.

Polymorphy and Specific Variations

Plants growing in the wild, even when confined to a very small locality, can show a wide range of habit, size and shape of leaves, flowers and other significant characteristics on which we rely for identification. This makes the positive identification of these plants that much more difficult. Those that have been introduced to a foreign country and that have been in cultivation for some time are, more often than not, the product of an individual, vegetatively propagated specimen, and are thus likely to have lost this richness of variety. In the wild the genus *Viburnum* shows an astonishing degree of variation, which leads to difficulties in identification with the result that many plants, which have been quoted as a species by one author, will be reduced to varietal rank or even mere synonymy by a later author.

It is abundantly clear that marked physical differences occur within the same species depending on where they are growing and particularly on the height above sea level. For shrubs and trees generally the habit diminishes in size with increase in altitude, leaves become smaller and of thicker texture, petioles become shorter, leaf base and apex tend to become more rounded and leaf margins tend to lose their serration, if any.

SECTIONS

To help in the classification of so widespread and diverse a genus it has been split into a number of distinct sections. This work was originally explained by Rehder in 1908 and remains relevant today, although two further sections have been added to Rehder's original nine.

Much of the formal classification within the various sections relies on a description of the stone of the fruit which is undoubtedly a most valuable indicator, although the number of grooves, if shallow, cannot always be easily determined nor indeed are the stones always available.

Particularly in relation to the Malaysian viburnums, the presence or absence of pitted glands on the leaves, especially of deep pits at the base of the leaf blade, is a further characteristic which merits greater attention.

Section Thyrsosma (Raf.) Rehd.

syn. Solenotinus DC.
      Microtinus (Oerst.) Hara
      Loniceroides (Oerst.) Hara
      Sieboldii (Nakai) Hara

Malecot (unpublished 1997) and Houtman (Dendroflora 35/1998) now quote this Section as **Solenotinus DC.**

Generally from the Himalaya and eastern Asia. With deciduous or evergreen leaves, the leaf petiole without stipules. The winter buds with 1-3 pairs of scales. The inflorescences paniculate or conical with opposite branching (often condensed in the winter-flowering species) with the corolla rotate to cylindric. The fruit ovoid to ellipsoid, blue-black or purple. The stone slightly compressed with a single deep furrow on the ventral side, the albumen solid or ruminate.

V. amplificatum Kern	Borneo
V. awabuki K Koch	Japan
V. brevitubum (Hsu) Hsu	China
V. brachybotryum Hemsl.	China
V. x bodnantense Stearn	Hort.
V. burmanicum (Rehd.) C.Y. Wu ex Hsu	Burma
V. carnosulum (W W Smith) Hsu	China
V. clemensae Kern	Borneo

V. chingii P S Hsu	W China (Yunnan)
V. corymbiflorum Hsu & S. C. Hsu	China
V. erubescens Wall.	Ceylon, India to China
V. farreri Stearn	China (Kansu)
V. grandiflorum Wall. ex DC.	Himalaya to W China
V. henryi Hemsl.	Central China (Hupeh)
V. x *hillieri* Stearn	Hort.
V. junghuhnii Miq.	Java
V. longipedunculatum (Hsu) Hsu	China
V. odoratissimum Ker-Gawl.	India, S E Asia and China
V. oliganthum Batal.	China
V. omeiense Hsu	China
V. shweliense W W Smith	W China (Yunnan)
V. sieboldii Miq.	Japan
V. subalpinum Hand.-Mazz.	China
V. suspensum Lindl.	Japan, Taiwan and Indonesia
V. taitoense Hayata	Taiwan
V. tengyuehense (W W Smith) Hsu	China
V. trabeculosum C Y Wu	China
V. tubulosum Hsu	China
V. wardii W W Smith	Burma
V. wightianum Wall.	China
V. yunnanense Rehd.	W China (Yunnan)

Section Lantana Spach.

Generally deciduous shrubs with naked winter buds and a stellate tomentum. The leaves toothed, some only slightly so. The flower trusses are corymbose without ray flowers (except *V. macrocephalum* (wild form)). The fruit are generally red turning to black or blue-black, the stone is distinctly flattened with three furrows on the ventral and two on the dorsal side (often indistinct), the albumen is solid.

V. bitchiuense Makino	S Japan and Korea
V. buddleifolium C H Wright	Central China
V. burejaeticum Regel & Herd.	N China, Korea and USSR
V. x *burkwoodii* Burk. & Skip. ex Anon.	Hort.
V. x *carlcephalum* Burk. & Skip.	Hort.
V. carlesii Hemsl.	Korea
V. cavaleriei Leville	China
V. chinshanense Graebn.	China
V. congestum Rehd.	China

V. cotonifolium D Don	Himalaya
V. fallax Graebn.	China
V. glomeratum Maxim.	China
V. x juddii Rehd.	Hort.
V. lantana L.	Europe
V. x lantanophyllum Lemoine	Hort
V. macrocephalum Fort.	China
V. mongolicum (Pall.) Rehd.	E Siberia
V. x rhytidocarpum Lemoine	Hort.
V. x rhytidophylloides Suringar	Hort.
V. rhytidophyllum Hemsl.	Central and W China
V. schensianum Maxim.	N-W China
V. urceolatum Sieb. & Zucc.	Japan
V. utile Hemsl.	China
V. veitchii C H Wright	Central China

Section Pseudotinus Clarke

Deciduous shrubs characterized by an indumentum of stellate hairs and winter buds naked or with a pair of caducous scales. Almost all are deciduous and the leaves are finely toothed, some only slightly so. The flower corymbs, often subsessile, are terminal, usually with enlarged sterile marginal flowers. The fruit are generally red turning to black or blue-black, the stone is compressed with a deeper furrow on the ventral side and the albumen is ruminate.

V. furcatum Bl.	Japan and Taiwan
V. lantanoides Michx.	E North America and Canada
V. nervosum D Don	E Himalaya, China to Taiwan
V. sympodiale Graebn.	Central China

Section Pseudopulus Dipp.

syn. Tomentosa Nakai
Euviburnum Oerst.

Deciduous shrubs, closely related to the Section Pseudotinus, with dentate leaves with straight veins running to the teeth and with stellate indumentum, estipulate. Winter buds have one pair of scales. Flowers in cymes with enlarged sterile marginal flowers at the end of short, lateral shoots. The fruit is purple-black, the stone compressed with a wide furrow on the ventral side and the albumen is solid.

V. plicatum Thunb.	China and Japan

Section Lentago (Raf.) DC.

Deciduous shrubs, the winter buds having one pair of scales. The leaves are either entire or finely serrate, the veins are bowed and anastomose before reaching the margin. The flower trusses are all fertile flowers. The fruit are blue-black or black, the stone is convex on the dorsal side with three shallow furrows on the ventral side and the albumen is solid.

V. cassinoides L.	E North America and Canada
V. x jackii Rehd.	Hort.
V. lentago L.	E North America and Canada
V. nudum L.	E North America
V. obovatum Walt.	E North America
V. prunifolium L.	E North America
V. rufidulum Raf.	S North America
V. x vetteri Zabel	Hort.

Section Tinus (Borkh.) Maxim.

syn. Viburnum Nicholson
      Tinus (Miller) C B Clarke
      Oreinotinus (Oerst.) Benth. & Hook.

All evergreen or semi-evergreen, usually glabrous, otherwise stellate-tomentose. The leaves are entire or indistinctly dentate, often three-veined from the base with secondary veins curved and anastomosing before reaching the margin. Petiole without stipules. Winter buds generally with one pair of scales or with four small scales. The corolla rotate. The fruit globose to ellipsoid, blue or blue-black, the stone without furrows or with one groove on the ventral side, and the albumen solid or slightly ruminate.

V. atrocyaneum C B Clarke	Assam
V. beccarii Gamble & King	Malaysia
V. calvum Rehd.	W China
V. cinnamomifolium Rehd.	W China (Mt. Omei)
V. davidii Franch.	W China
V. glabratum H B & K.	Colombia
V. x globosum Coombes	Hort.
V. harryanum Rehd.	China
V. hispidulum Kern	Borneo
V. inopinatum Craib	Burma
V. propinquum Hemsl.	Central and W China
V. rigidum Vent.	Canary Islands

V. sambucinum Reinw. ex Bl.	Malaysia
V. tinus L.	S Europe and N Africa
V. triplinerve Hand.-Mazz.	China (Kwangsi)

Section Megalotinus (Maxim.) Rehd.

Evergreen shrubs with winter buds having one pair of outer scales. The leaves are entire or finely dentate, pinnately veined, the veins diverting before reaching the margin. The petiole without stipules. The corolla rotate or cylindric-campanulate. The fruit blue-black or purple, the stone compressed with two dorsal and one ventral furrow and the albumen usually solid.

V. cylindricum Buch.-Ham. ex D Don	S-E Asia to China
V. inopinatum Craib	Burma
V. leiocarpum Hsu	W China (Yunnan)
V. pyramidatum Rehd.	W China (Yunnan)
V. ternatum Rehd.	W China

For the classification of the Malaysian viburnums Kern has suggested the expansion of the section Megalotinus into four distinct sub-sections:

Coriacea (Maxim.) Kern

Corolla tubular, filaments twisted.

V. beccarii Gamble & King	Sumatra and Malay Peninsula
V. coriaceum Bl.	Himalaya and Malaysia
V. cornutidens Merr.	Philippines
V. glaberrimum Merr.	Philippines
V. platyphyllum Merr.	Philippines (Leyte)

Lutescentia Kern

Leaves serrate, filaments short and twisted

V. lutescens Bl.	Malaysia and W China

Punctata Kern

Young parts covered with small, scurfy scales, filaments twisted.

V. punctatum Buch.-Ham. ex D Don	Malaysia and W China

Sambucina Kern

Leaves entire, filaments long, serpentiform.

V. hispidulum Kern	Borneo
V. sambucinum Reinw. ex Blume	Malaysia
V. vernicosum Gibbs	Borneo

Section Odontotinus Rehd.

Generally deciduous shrubs with winter buds having two or three pairs of scales. The leaves are usually dentate with straight lateral veins running out to the teeth, occasionally diverting before reaching the margin and, again occasionally, the leaves are three-veined and lobed. The petiole with or without stipules. The corolla rotate and the inflorescence corymbose with umbellate rays. All the Asiatic species have bright red fruits, although those of *V. ovatifolium* turn almost black when ripe, whereas those of the American species have fruits which are blue-black. The stone has three or one ventral and two (often indistinct) dorsal furrows and the albumen is solid.

V. acerifolium L.	E North America
V. affine Bush ex Rehd.	North America
V. betulifolium Batal.	Central and W China
V. bracteatum Rehd.	S-E North America
V. brevipes Rehd.	China
V. carolinum Ashe	North America (Carolina)
V. chunii Hsu	China
V. colebrookeanum Wall	Himalaya
V. corylifolium Hook. f. & Thoms.	E Himalaya and W China
V. crenatum McAtee	North America (Indiana)
V. dazielii W W Smith	China
V. dasyanthum Rehd.	Central and W China
V. dentatum L.	E North America
V. dilatatum Thunb.	Japan and China
V. ellipticum Hook.	N-W North America
V. erosum Thunb.	Japan and China
V. flavescens W W Smith	China (Yunnan)
V. foetidum Wall.	Himalaya, China and Taiwan
V. fordiae Hance	China
V. formosanum (Maxim.) Hayata	Taiwan
V. hainanense Merr. & Chun	China (Hainan)
V. hanceanum (Maxim.)	China
V. hengshanicum Tsiang & Hsu	China

V. x *hizense* Hatus.	Japan
V. hupehense Rehd.	China (Hupeh and Sichuan)
V. ichangense Rehd.	China (Hupeh)
V. indianense (Rehd.)McAtee	North America
V. integrifolium Hayata	Taiwan
V. japonicum (Thunb.)Spreng.	Japan and Taiwan
V. kansuense Batal.	W China
V. lancifolium Hsu	China
V. lobophyllum Graebn.	Central and W China
V. longiradiatum Hsu & S W Fan	China (Sichuan and Yunnan)
V. luzonicum Rolfe	Philippines, China and Taiwan
V. melanocarpum Hsu	China
V. molle Michx.	Central and S North America
V. mullaha Buch.-Ham. ex D Don	Himalaya and S-E Asia
V. orientale Pall.	Caucasus and Asia Minor
V. ovatifolium Rehd.	Yunnan
V. ozarkense Ashe	North America (Arkansas)
V. parvifolium Hayata	China and Taiwan
V. phlebotrichum Sieb. & Zucc.	Japan
V. rafinesquianum Schult.	E North America and Canada
V. recognitum Fern.	North America
V. scabrellum (T & G) Chapm.	North America
V. sempervirens K Koch	China and Malaysia
V. setigerum Hance	Central and W China
V. squamulosum Hsu	China
V. wilsonii Rehd.	Central and W China
V. wrightii Miq.	Japan and Korea

Section Opulus DC.

Deciduous shrubs, the winter buds having a pair of connate outer scales. The leaves are three- or five-veined from the base, usually three-lobed and with stipules at the base of the petiole; they are generally glabrous or pubescent with simple hairs. The inflorescence corymbose, often with enlarged sterile marginal flowers. The fruit are red or scarlet, the stone is flat without a furrow or only slightly furrowed.

Hara differentiates two Groups within this Section, one with large sterile marginal flowers and stipulate petioles with discoid glands near the apex (*V. opulus, sargentii* and *trilobum*), the other without sterile marginal flowers, with less lobed leaves and with petioles sometimes estipulate and also without glands (*V. edule* and *koreanum*).

He also considers that *V. kansuense* should be included in Section Odontotinus and not Opulus as it has two pairs of separate coriaceous scales and the stones are grooved.

V. edule (Michx.) Raf.	North America
V. kansuense Batal.	China
V. koreanum Nakai	Korea
V. opulus L.	Europe
V. sargentii Koehne	N-E Asia
V. trilobum Marsh	North America

Section Oreinotinus (Oerst.) Benth. & Hook.

Evergreen shrubs from tropical America, the buds with two pairs of scales. The leaves stellate-tomentose or glabrous, entire or dentate, the lateral veins of the leaves are straightish or slightly curved, simple or forked to the teeth, sometimes stipulate. The inflorescence corymbose with umbellate rays, mostly flat-topped (but globose in snowball forms). The drupe is red or black and the stone compressed with one ventral groove, the albumen solid or slightly ruminate.

Stipulata
V. australe Morton	Mexico

Sessilia
V. elatum Benth.	Mexico

Bracteata
V. guatemalense Gandoger	Guatemala
V. hartwegi Benth.	Mexico and Guatemala

Costaricana
V. conspectum Morton	Panama
V. costaricanum (Oerst.) Hemsl.	Costa Rica
V. venustum Morton	Costa Rica

Mexicana
V. acutifolium Benth.	Mexico
V. amatemangense Lundell	Mexico
V. blandum Morton	Mexico
V. dispar Morton	Mexico
V. fuscum (Oerst.) Hemsl.	Mexico

V. lautum Morton	Mexico
V. microphyllum (Oerst.) Hemsl.	Mexico
V. subpubescens Lundell	Honduras

Disjuncta

V. chiapense Lundell	Mexico
V. discolor Benth.	Guatemala
V. disjunctum Morton	Guatemala
V. hondurense Standl.	Honduras
V. jucundum Morton	Guatemala
V. stellato-tomentosum (Oerst.) Hemsl.	Costa Rica
V. sulcatum (Oerst.) Hemsl.	Mexico

Optata

V. molinae Lundell	Honduras
V. optatum Morton	Guatemala
V. siltepecanum Lundell	Mexico

Ciliata

V. ciliatum Greenm.	Mexico
V. membranaceum (Oerst.) Hemsl.	Mexico

Caudata

V. caudatum Greenm.	Mexico

Serrata

V. hirsutum Morton	Mexico
V. loeseneri Graebn.	Mexico
V. microcarpum Schlect. & Cham.	Mexico
V. rhombifolium (Oerst.) Hemsl.	Mexico
V. stenocalyx (Oerst.) Hemsl.	Mexico
V. tiliaefolium (Oerst.) Hemsl.	Mexico

Others

V. ayavacense H B & K.	Peru
V. cornifolium Killip & Smith	Colombia
V. divaricatum Benth.	Peru
V. floccosum Killip & Smith	Colombia
V. fragile Killip & Smith	Colombia
V. glabratum H B & K.	Colombia
V. halli (Oerst.) Killip & Smith	Colombia and Ecuador
V. jamesonii (Oerst.) Killip & Smith	Colombia
V. lasiophyllum Benth.	Colombia

V. lehmannii Killip & Smith	Colombia
V. leptophyllum Killip & Smith	Colombia
V. mathewsii (Oerst.) Killip & Smith	Peru
V. pinchinchense Benth.	Bolivia, Colombia and Ecuador
V. stellatum (Oerst.) Hemsl.	Mexico
V. suratense Killip & Smith	Colombia
V. tinoides L.	South America
V. toronis Killip & Smith	Colombia
V. triphyllum Benth.	Colombia
V. undulatum (Oerst.) Killip & Smith	Colombia and Venezuela
V. villosum Swart	Tropical South America

Section Platyphylla Hsu

A new Section proposed by P S Hsu to accommodate just two species. The winter buds have one pair of scales. The leaves are serrate with some of the lateral veins running out directly to the teeth, estipulate. The inflorescences terminal in umbellate cymes on second-year branches. The drupe red, the stone compressed with one shallow groove on the dorsal side and two on the ventral side.

V. amplifolium Rehd.	W China (Yunnan)
V. laterale Rehd.	China

Not included in any Section

V. albopedunculatum Gilli	Papua New Guinea
V. anabaptista Graebn.	Colombia
V. annamensis Fukuoka	Vietnam
V. antioquiense Killip & Smith	Colombia
V. arboreum Britton	Jamaica
V. austrokoreanum Nakai	Korea
V. brachyandrum Nakai	Japan
V. brunnescens Standl. & Steyerm.	Guatemala
V. canum Friff.	Bhutan
V. cornutidens Merr.	Philippines
V. cuttingianum Merr.	Borneo
V. delicatulum Vatke	Montenegro
V. deltoideum M E Jones	N South America
V. euryphyllum Stand. & Steyerm.	Guatemala
V. garettii Craib	Burma
V. goudotii Killip & Smith	Colombia

V. griffithianum C B Clarke	East Assam
V. hebanthum Wight & Arnold	Himalaya
V. incarum Graebn.	Peru
V. jelskii Zahlbr.	Ecuador and Peru
V. kanbok Sieb.	Japan
V. kerrii Geddes	Thailand
V. x *kiusianum* Hatus.	Japan
V. macdougallii Matuda	Mexico
V. maculatum Pantocsek	Balkan Peninsula
V. matudae Morton	Mexico
V. meiothyrsum Diels	Peru
V. montanum Lundell	Mexico
V. mortonianum Standl. & Steyerm.	Guatemala
V. x *multratum* Hort. ex K Koch	Hort.
V. obtusatum D Gibson	Mexico
V. pastasanum Diels	Ecuador
V. peruvianum MacBride	Peru
V. pubescens (Ait.) Pursh.	North America
V. queremalense Cuatrec.	Colombia
V. seemenii Graebn.	Bolivia
V. simonsii Hook. & Arn.	India
V. spruceanum Rusby	Bolivia
V. subsessile Killip & Smith	Colombia
V. tacanense Lundell	Mexico
V. thaiyongense W W Smith	China
V. thibeticum C Y Wu & Y F Huang	Tibet
V. tricostatum C E C Fischer	Burma
V. tridentatum Killip & Smith	Peru
V. trileasi Gand.	Azores
V. urbani Graebn.	Colombia
V. viride Kern ex Degen	E Europe
V. weberbaueri Graebn.	Peru
V. wurdackii T R Dudley	Peru
V. xanthoneurum Diels	Ecuador
V. zeylandicum Gardn.	Himalaya and Malaya

CATALOGUE

***Viburnum acerifolium* L.** ❀ Sp. Pl. 268 (1753)

The maple leaf viburnum or dockmackie.

A medium sized deciduous shrub from E North America and Canada from Minnesota to Ontario, of suckering habit growing to 1-2 metres with a similar spread with straight, slender grey-brown branches, *V. acerifolium* grows well in dry, acid woodland conditions. The leaves are maple-like, three lobed (the younger leaves do not always show the side lobes), the side lobes closer to the tip than a maple and with divergent slender points all coarsely toothed, rounded or cordate at the base, 4-10cm long and the same wide. Dull mid-green, pubescent on both sides, more densely so on the underside turning to yellow, pinkish-red and finally a rich dark maroon in autumn, often several colours are on one leaf at the same time. The petiole is slender, 1-2cm long, slightly downy with one or two pairs of stipules up to 8mm long at the base. The flowers borne in May or June are all uniform and fertile, pale purple in bud opening to pure white 5mm in diameter, in terminal long-stalked 3-7 rayed trusses 5-8cm across. The fruit are bright red turning purplish-black in autumn, about 8mm long and oval.

A yellow-fruited variety was reported in New York (AmHort 1962) but is now believed to be lost.

***V. acerifolium* f. *collinsii* Rouleau** A form with pink rather than the usual creamy-white petals; reported from South Ontario by Gaiser & Moore (1966).

***V. acerifolium* f. *eburneum* House** A white-fruiting form.

***V. acerifolium* f. *glabrescens* Rehd.** Glabrous, except along the veins.

***V. acerifolium* f. *ovatum* Rehd.** Some or all of the leaves are two-lobed, have short lobes, or are unlobed becoming ovate. Remotely dentate and subcordate at the base.

***Viburnum atrocyaneum* C B Clarke** ❀ Hook. f. Fl. Brit. Ind. iii.7 (1880)

A small evergreen shrub growing to about 1 metre high and the same or more across from the Himalaya. The leaves are oblong or ovate, narrowed at both ends, not acuminate at the apex, entire or obscurely sinuate-dentate, with 5-7 pairs of pinnate veins 4-6cm long, 3-4cm wide. The leaves are purplish when young turning dark green in summer and reverting to a bronze-green in winter, completely glabrous without hairs even in the vein-axils beneath. The petiole is short, 7-10mm long, deep maroon whilst the midrib beneath is maroon towards the base gradually changing to green towards the apex. The inflorescences are insignificant with only a few flowers in terminal sub-sessile cymes borne in late May, but this is compensated for by the fruit which is a shiny steel-blue, elliptic and 4mm long.

Viburnum awabuki **K Koch** ❀ Wochenschr. x:109 (1899)

syn. *V. odoratissimum* sensu auct. Japon, non Ker.-Gawl., *V. odoratissimum* var. *uwubuki* (K. Koch) K. Koch ex Ruempler

Taxonomists argue as to whether or not this is a synonym for *V. odoratissimum* or at least its Japanese form. However there are significant differences noted between the two forms, whereas *V. odoratissimum* has smooth-barked branches and thin elliptic-ovate leaves, *V. awabuki* has stout, lenticular branches and thicker leaves tending to be more obovate; the axillary buds of *V. awabuki* are more prominent. In the flowers there are further differences noticeable, namely that in the Japanese form the corolla tube is longer and the lobes are relatively shorter.

An evergreen shrub from the lowland areas of Japan, eastern China and Taiwan where it is frequently planted as a hedge, growing to 3-8 metres with a spread up to 5 metres. The leaves are elliptic-ovate to obovate or oblong, obtuse or acute at both ends, entire or sometimes undulately short-toothed on the upper half, with 6-8 pairs of upwardly directed lateral veins, 8-16cm long, 5-10cm wide, lustrous above, paler beneath and glabrous. The petiole is stout, 2.5-4cm long. The flowers borne in May and June are pure white, 6mm in diameter, fragrant, all perfect in wide panicles 6-12cm across. The fruit are red, ellipsoidal, 7-8mm long.

V. awabuki **'Chindo'**   A selection introduced from Korea to North America by J C Raulston, said to be more reliable in flower and fruit.

Viburnum betulifolium **Batal.** ❀ Act. Hort. Petrop. xiii. 371 (1894)

syn. *Viburnum morrisonense* Hayata

The birch-leaved viburnum. Introduced by Wilson in 1901. AM 1936, FCC 1957, AGM (1960).

A deciduous shrub of bushy habit from western and central China and Taiwan, closely related to *V. lobophyllum*, growing to 3-5 metres with a spread of 2-3 metres. The leaves ovate or rhombic-ovate, sometimes elliptic-oblong, gradually tapering at the apex, wedge-shaped at the base, coarsely toothed except near the base with 4-5 pairs of veins, 5-10cm long by 4-8cm wide, dark green and glabrous above, greyer beneath, sparingly hairy on the veins and bearded in the vein-axils. The petiole 1-2cm long, slender and usually slightly hairy with small stipules. The flowers borne in June and July are in short-stalked, rather loose corymbs 6-10cm across composed of small white flowers 5mm across, usually 7-rayed. The fruit are globose-ellipsoid, bright red about 6mm long. Plants may take some years to berry, but fruit abundantly when older, especially if the viburnums are planted in groups of plants of different clones.

V. betulifolium f. *auranticum* **Rehd.** ❀ A yellow-fruited variety, considered possibly to have been lost but listed as growing at the Royal Botanic Garden, Edinburgh.

V. betulifolium var. *flocculosum* **(Rehd.) Hsu**   Alive at Kew.

V. betulifolium '**Marchant**'   Growing at Hyde Hall August 1999. Appears to have a smaller leaf and pinkish fruit.

V. betulifolium '**Trewithen**' is a particularly good fruiting cultivar selected by G H Johnstone of Trewithen.

Viburnum bitchiuense **Makino** ❀ Bot. Mag. Tokyo xvi.156

syn. *V. carlesii* var. *bitchiuense* (Makino) Nakai, *V. carlesii* var. *syringaefolia* Hutchins, *V. burejaeticum* sensu auct. Japon, non Regel & Herder, *Solenolantana carlesii* var. *bitchiuensis* (Makino) Nakai.

Very similar to *V. carlesii* but with narrower leaves, growing taller and of more open habit.   Indeed when it was introduced from Japan in 1911 it was initially mistaken for a form of *V. carlesii*, but the clusters of flowers are much looser than those of *V. carlesii*. AGM (1948).

A deciduous shrub from southern Japan and Korea growing to 2-3 metres with a similar spread. The leaves are ovate to oblong, acute at the apex, sometimes slightly heart-shaped at the base, 3-8cm long, 2-5cm wide, dull dark bluish-green above, lighter beneath, turning dull red in autumn. The petiole light green, 8-12mm long. The flowers borne in April and May are pink at first, turning white, sweetly scented in loose cymes up to 7cm across. The corolla nearly 1cm wide, the tube very narrow, 8mm long. The fruit are flattened ovoid, about 6mm long turning black when ripe.

Viburnum **x** *bodnantense* **Stearn** ❀ Bot. Mag. Lond. clxvii.t.113 (1950)

A family of hybrids between *V. farreri* and *V. grandiflorum*, valuable for their profusion of fragrant flowers borne on naked branches in the winter months. The original hybridization was carried out by Charles Lamont in 1933 when he was Assistant Curator at the Royal Botanic Garden, Edinburgh, with *V. grandiflorum* as the seed parent. At the time he did not consider that the cross was any improvement on the parents and so did not propagate them.   The following year the opposite cross, i.e. *V. farreri* pollinated by *V. grandiflorum*, was raised by Charles Puddle, head gardener to Lord Aberconway at Bodnant.

26

From the ten seedlings Puddle selected one, 'Dawn', which received the Award of Merit in 1947 and the Award of Garden Merit in 1960. In reviewing his seedlings Lamont found one worthy of propagation which is now named 'Charles Lamont' and is a brighter pink and said to be more freely flowering than 'Dawn'.

A third cultivar, 'Deben', was raised from a chance seedling by Messrs R C Notcutt Ltd and received an Award of Merit in 1962 and a First Class Certificate in 1965. The flowers are whiter than 'Dawn' but more prone to damage by the weather.

A strongly suckering deciduous shrub growing to 3 metres or more with a spread of 2 metres. The leaves are narrowly oval to ovate, tapered towards both ends, finely and regularly toothed, 5-10cm long by 2.5-5cm wide, purplish when young turning dull green through the summer, colouring well in autumn. The petiole bright red, 2cm long. The flowers are borne on the naked winter branches between December and March in small cymes 4-5cm across by 2.5-3cm high, branching once with seven or eight short primary rays 6-8mm long, slightly hairy, rose-red in bud, becoming bright pink, the individual flowers up to 10mm in diameter lightening as they open but never becoming fully white. Corolla trumpet-shaped, 10mm long, anthers shorter than the corolla, style about 1mm long. The fruit are narrow oval, 5-8mm long, red turning blackish-purple when ripe.

V. x *bodnantense* **'Charles Lamont'** ❀ Flowers slightly larger and more intense pink than those of 'Dawn', and with yellow anthers. Flowering reliably from a young age. AGM 1993.

V. x *bodnantense* **'Dawn'** ❀ Pink flowers with dark purple-pink anthers. AM 1947, AGM (1960)1993.

V. x *bodnantense* **'Deben'** ❀ Extra large individual flowers opening pale apple-blossom pink rapidly fading to pure white. Possibly a cross with *V. farreri* 'Candidissimum' rather than the pink-flowered type. AM 1962, FCC 1965, AGM (1969)1993.

Viburnum bracteatum **Rehd.** ❀ Sargent, Trees and Shrubs, 135 (1908)

Introduced in about 1904. Closely related to *V. dentatum* and *V. rafinesquianum*, the specific epithet refers to the distinctive bracts on the stems of the flower trusses below the flowers.

A deciduous shrub from the south-eastern United States growing to 3 metres with the same spread. The leaves are circular to ovate, bluntly pointed at the apex, rounded or cuneate at the base, coarsely sinuately dentate with 5-6 pairs of parallel veins ending at the tips of the teeth, 5-12cm long by 3.5-8cm wide, dark glossy green and glabrous above except for a few hairs on the mid-rib, paler beneath with hairs on the veins and in the vein-axils. The petiole 15-20mm long, pubescent. The flowers borne in May-June are in cymes 4-8cm across with distinct bracts. The fruit are ovoid, 10mm long turning blue-black when ripe.

V. bracteatum '**Emerald Luster**' Named by Michael Dirr at the University of Georgia, Atlanta Botanic Garden. Bright green leaves with pubescence on buds and stems.

Viburnum buddleifolium **C H Wright** ❀ Gard. Chron. I.257 (1903)

Introduced by Wilson in 1900.

A gracefully branched, deciduous or semi-evergreen mound-shaped shrub from central China, with pale green velvety textured leaves, growing to 2 metres with a similar spread. The leaves oblong-lanceolate, pointed at apex, rounded or slightly heart shaped at base. Shallowly toothed with 8-10 vein-pairs, the veins forming a deep groove on the upper surface and conspicuously raised beneath. The young shoots are densely covered with pale star-like down, 15-20cm long by 3-5cm wide, pale green, softly pubescent above, grey felted beneath. The petiole, short in comparison with the length of the blade, up to 1cm long. The flowers borne in May-June are white, funnel shaped 8mm across, all perfect, produced on a short stalked, 7-rayed compound cymes 6-10cm across, light pink in bud opening white with prominent anthers. The fruit are oval, 8mm long, red at first turning to black.

Viburnum burejaeticum **Regel & Herder** ❀ Gartenfl. 407 (1862)

Named after the Bureia mountains in China, introduced in about 1900.

A deciduous shrub from N China, Korea and E USSR, growing to 4-5 metres with almost the same spread, the young shoots are covered in a dense stellate down which they lose in the following year revealing an almost white bark. The leaves are oval, ovate or slightly obovate, tapered to the apex, rounded or slightly heart-shaped at the base, finely toothed, 5-10cm long by 3-5cm wide, light green with a few hairs above, more beneath especially on the veins, but losing these as the leaves age. The petiole 3-8mm long, scurfy pubescent. The flowers borne in May are all perfect, white, in dense 5-rayed cymes 4-5cm across, each flower 6mm in diameter, the flower stalks covered in down. The fruit are ellipsoid, 10mm long and black.

Viburnum x *burkwoodii* **Burkw. & Skip. ex Anon.** ❀ Gard. Chron.
85:285 (1929)

A hybrid from *V. utile* pollinated by *V. carlesii* raised by Burkwood & Skipwith
in Kingston-on-Thames in 1924. Very hardy and easily propagated from
cuttings, it is tolerant of polluted atmospheres. AM 1929, AGM (1956)

An almost evergreen shrub growing to 2.5 metres high and the same across. The
leaves are ovate, pointed at the apex, rounded or slightly heart-shaped at the
base and indistinctly toothed, 4-10cm long by 2-4cm wide, bright shiny green
above, thickly covered with pale down beneath. Although mainly evergreen,
the older leaves may colour before dropping in autumn. The petiole short,
6mm or less. The highly fragrant flowers borne in April and May are in
rounded trusses 6-9cm across, each flower about 12mm across. Pinkish when
young, turning pure white. The fruit are oval, 6-8mm long, turning black when ripe.

V. x *burkwoodii* 'Chenaultii' ❀ Raised in France as the same cross and originally known
as *V.* x *chenaultii*, has a more compact growth and finer textured leaves and the flower
buds are almost white, rather than pink as in the type.

V. x *burkwoodii* 'Conoy' ❀ Introduced by the US National Arboretum in 1988, 'Conoy' is
a selection from the cross of *V. utile* with *V.* x *burkwoodii* 'Park Farm Hybrid'. It has a more
compact habit, fine-textured, evergreen foliage and more persistent and abundant glossy
red fruit which last for 6-8 weeks. Frequently mis-named as 'Conroy'.

V. x *burkwoodii* 'Fulbrook' ❀ A more vigorous shrub than the type. AM 1957, AGM
(1984)1993.

V. x *burkwoodii* 'Fulbrook Pink' Exhibited RHS by Mrs Douglas Gordon April 1957.
Possibly no longer in cultivation.

V. x *burkwoodii* 'Park Farm Hybrid' ❀ Raised in 1924 at the same time as the original
cross. Not as tall and of broader habit than the original cross with leaves more ovate to
lanceolate, 7-10cm long, entire or slightly serrate. The flower clusters are larger, 10-12cm
across and pinker in the bud. Has been known to flower from February to May. AM 1949,
AGM 1993.

Because of its success as a gardenworthy plant, much hybridization has been
practised, the most successful being the back-crosses with *V. carlesii*. The greater
proportion of this parent, which is itself deciduous renders these plants
deciduous, or almost so, with the added benefit of some spectacular autumn
shades of brilliant reds, oranges and yellows.

V. (x *burkwoodii* x *carlesii*) 'Anne Russell' ❀ Usually referred to as *V.* x *burkwoodii* 'Anne
Russell'. Selected by John Russell of L R Russell Ltd, Richmond Nurseries, Windlesham
and named after his wife. Selected for its noticeably heavy textured foliage and upright

habit. The flowers open several weeks before those of 'Fulbrook'. AM 1957, AGM (1984)1993.

V. **(x** *burkwoodii* **x** *carlesii)* **'Carlotta'** syn. *V. x carlotta*. Introduced as a seedling of *V. x burkwoodii* by W B Clarke & Co, San Jose, California and described as an improved *V. carlesii*, but no longer propagated by the nursery.

V. **(x** *burkwoodii* **x** *carlesii)* **'Mohawk'** ❀ Developed at the US National Arboretum in 1960 by Dr Donald Egolf and released in 1966. Seedling production was expedited by embryo-culture.

V. **(x** *burkwoodii* **x** *carlesii)* **'Sarcoxie'** The result of a controlled pollination in 1971 and introduced by Dale E Wild of Sarcoxie Nursery in 1976. Mr Wild originally tried to register the name as 'Bur-Carl' which was mercifully rejected by the International Registration Authority. Upright in youth more rounded in age. With fragrant flowers in trusses 5-8cm across.

Viburnum calvum **Rehd.** Sargent, Pl. Wilson i:310 (1912)

A fine textured shrub with compact growth, introduced by Wilson in 1904 but not common in cultivation in the British Isles.

An evergreen shrub from western China growing to 2-2.5 metres high with the same spread. The leaves are narrowly ovate to rhombic-elliptic, pointed at the apex, heart-shaped at the base, entire or with a few teeth, with 5-8 pairs of veins deeply impressed above, 4-8cm long by 3-5cm wide, dull grey-green above, pale beneath. The petiole short, up to 10mm long. The flowers borne in May in cymes 5-8cm across of white or creamy-white flowers. The fruit globose-ovoid, 6mm long, lustrous blue-black when ripe.

Viburnum **x** *carlcephalum* **Burkw. & Skipw. ex A. V. Pike** ❀

A hybrid between *V. carlesii* (seed parent) and *V. macrocephalum* f. *keteleeri* raised by Albert Burkwood of Messrs Burkwood & Skipwith in 1932, which came to popularity after receiving an Award of Merit in 1946. Very similar to *V. carlesii*, being distinguished by the leaves which are larger and slightly glossy, and the flower trusses which are also larger but not as numerous. The flowers are not as fragrant as those of *V. carlesii*, *V. bitchiuense* or *V. x juddii*. AM 1946, AGM (1964)1993.

A deciduous shrub growing to 2.5 metres with the same spread, the leaves broadly ovate, sometimes with a slightly heart shaped base, 4-10cm long by 3-6cm wide, slightly glossy green above, greyish below, often colouring richly in autumn. The petiole about 1cm long. The flowers borne in May in dense rounded corymbs of fragrant flowers up to 15cm across with up to 100 flowers, all fertile, in each truss. Pink in bud, white when open. The fruit a flattened egg shape up to 1cm long, jet black.

V. x *carlcephalum* 'Cayuga' ❀ A backcross selection distinguished by a more compact growth than the type, the foliage is a darker green and the inflorescences are more abundant; the veins on the underside turning maroon in autumn.

V. x *carlcephalum* 'Variegatum' ❀ A variegated form, growing more weakly than the type.

Amongst the introductions by Dr Donald Egolf of the US National Arboretum are two well known crosses with *V. utile*:

Viburnum (x *carlcephalum* 'Cayuga' x *utile*) 'Chesapeake' ❀ A semi-evergreen shrub with narrowly ovate to oblong leaves, darker and glossy green above with pink buds opening to white, the flowers in May or early June only slightly fragrant.

Viburnum (x *carlcephalum* 'Cayuga' x *utile*) 'Eskimo' ❀ A dense, compact, semi-evergreen form introduced by the US National Arboretum in 1981; the flowers trusses are pure white, almost perfectly spherical and larger than those of 'Chesapeake'.

Viburnum carlesii Hemsl. ❀ Journ. Linn. Soc. xxiii.350 (1888)

Syn. *Solenolantana carlesii* (Hemsl.) Nakai

Originally described from dried specimens which were collected by W R Carles and Wykeham Perry in 1885 in Western Korea, the first live specimen was sent to Kew in 1901 from the nursery of L Boehmer & Co in Yokohama and flowered in 1906.

Often unnecessarily grafted or budded onto *V. lantana* or *V. rhytidophyllum* rootstock. It is therefore imperative to keep an eye out for suckering which will take over in such cases. AM 1908, FCC 1909, AGM (1923).

A deciduous shrub from Korea and Tsushima Island, Japan, growing to 2 metres with the same spread, the leaves ovate, pointed at the apex and heart-shaped at the base, irregularly toothed and with 5-6 vein-pairs breaking into several veins each before they reach the margin, 3-8cm long by 2-5cm wide, dull green above, greyish below, both sides covered with a hairy down, often turning bright red in autumn. The petiole about 6mm long, grooved and hairy. The flowers borne in April-May very fragrant in terminal rounded clusters 5-8cm across composed of all fertile flowers each up to 1cm diameter. Early spring buds are a reddish brown becoming deep pink before opening to white tinged with pink. The fruit flattened ovoid, 8mm long and jet black.

Leslie Slinger of the Slieve Donard Nursery, County Down, Ireland (ceased trading in 1976) constantly tried to improve *V. carlesii*. In about 1950 he imported seed from Japan and, by painstaking selection, cross-fertilization and reselection, introduced three cultivars in 1958.

V. carlesii **'Aurora'** ❀ Flowers much more red in bud, opening to pink before turning white, but when open the flowers are the whitest. The leaves a lighter green sometimes flushed with copper. Very fragrant. AGM (1964)1993.

V. carlesii **'Charis'** ❀ A more vigorous form with the most open habit, the leaves, which are yellowish when young, and the inflorescences are the largest of all the three cultivars.

V. carlesii **'Diana'** ❀ A vigorous form with flower clusters up to 10cm across, red or deep pink in bud opening to white flushed with pink.

Other cultivars include:

V. carlesii **'Compactum'** ❀ A dwarf form.

V. carlesii **'Marlou'** ❀ Introduced by Ward van Teylingen, Boskoop, Netherlands.

V. carlesii **'Variegata'** A slow-growing variegated form.

Viburnum cassinoides **L.** ❀ Sp. Pl. ed. II, 284 (1753)

syn. *V. squamatum* Muhl. ex Willd.
The withe-rod, swamp or Appalachian tea viburnum, swamp black-haw, false Paraguay tea or wild raisin, introduced in about 1761.
The stems, which are smooth or brown-scurfy, were used as canes by pioneer teachers in country schools. Prefers a moist acid soil, a native of swampy regions in thickets or on the borders of woods.

A deciduous suckering shrub from eastern North America and Canada growing to 2.5 metres high with almost the same spread. The leaves are ovate to oval with a short, slender, often bluntish apex, rounded or wedge-shaped at the base. Irregularly and shallowly round-toothed or merely wavy at the margin, 3-10cm long by 2-6cm wide, chocolate or bronze-tinted when young, turning to dull dark green and glabrous above, somewhat scurfy beneath, turning bright orange-red in autumn before they fall. The petiole pink, slightly winged, 8-20mm long. The flowers borne in May or early June are all uniform and perfect, yellowish white 5-6 mm in diameter in cymes 5-10cm across, the main stalk being shorter than the branching stems. The fruit ovoid to nearly round, 8-10mm long, green turning pink or red and finally blue-black when ripe with different colours of fruit appearing in the same cluster.

V. cassinoides 'Nanum' ❀ A dwarf distorted form with crinkled leaves.

Viburnum chingii P S Hsu ❀ Acta Phytotax. Sin. xi.68 (1966)

An evergreen shrub from China growing to 5 metres high. The leaves are oval with a bluntish apex, more tapered at the base, regularly toothed, 4-6cm long by 1.5-3cm wide, reddish-bronze when young turning dull mid-green above, lighter beneath, the central vein reddish for up to half its length. The petiole 8-10mm long, glossy red. The flowers borne in April-May in small cymes up to 5cm across and the same in length, all perfect, pink in bud and when first opening, then fading to white, each 6-8mm in diameter, the corolla tube 6-8mm long. The tips of the petals curving right back on themselves. The fruit an oblate spheroid, 7-8mm long, black when ripe.

Viburnum cinnamomifolium Rehd. ❀ Sargent, Trees and Shrubs ii..31 (1908)

Introduced by Wilson from China in 1904. Very similar to *V. davidii*, but a much taller shrub with attractive reddish-brown branches and prominent pedicels which remain on the stems long after the berries have been taken by birds. AGM 1993.

An evergreen shrub from Mt. Omei and elsewhere in W Sichuan, China, growing to 4-6 metres with the same spread. The leaves are narrowly oval, slightly obovate or elliptic-oblong, slenderly tapered at the tip, less so or cuneate at the base. Conspicuously three-veined from the base, nearly entire, or shallowly toothed near the apex 5-15cm long by 3-6cm wide, less leathery than those of *V. davidii*, glossy dark green above, paler beneath with small tufts of down in the vein-axils beneath. The petiole thickish, greenish-pink to red, 1-2.5cm long. The flowers borne in May-June in loose, long-stalked terminal, 7-rayed cymes 12-15cm wide of creamy white perfect flowers 3-4mm in diameter on rays of the third order. The fruit ovate or ovoid, 4-6mm long by 3-4mm in diameter, glossy dark turquoise-blue.

Viburnum congestum Rehd. ❀ Sargent, Trees and Shrubs ii.111 (1908)

Very similar to *V. utile* which differs in the larger corolla which is almost rotate, the inflorescence is larger and more lax and the tomentum is mingled with yellowish scales.
An evergreen shrub from Mengtze, Yunnan about 1.3 metres high, the branchlets keeping

a dense whitish stellate-tomentose covering until the third year. The leaves oval to elliptic-ovate, obtuse or acute at the apex, rounded or broadly cuneate at the base, entire, strong green above at first sparsely stellate-pubescent but soon becoming glabrous, covered beneath in a ashen-white or yellowish-white tomentum, 2-4cm long. Petiole densely tomentose, 5-10mm long. Terminal and lateral corymbs, dense and small, 2-3cm in diameter the peduncle stellate-tomentose, 5-10mm long, with 5 short angular stellate-tomentose rays. Flowers white, sub-sessile on first and second order rays, calyces with short teeth and broad ovate and, together with the ovary, glabrous. Corolla campanulate funnel shaped, white, 5mm long and glabrous, lobes orbiculate-ovate, the tube about half the length.

Viburnum corylifolium **Hook. f. & Thoms.** Journ. Linn. Soc. ii:174 (1858)

An upright shrub with densely pubescent young shoots and large fruiting corymbs, similar to *V. dilatatum* from which it is distinguished by the long rust-brown pubescence. Introduced in 1907.

A deciduous shrub from the eastern Himalaya and W China growing to 2-3 metres with the same spread. The leaves are nearly circular to obovate or elliptic, abruptly short acuminate at the apex, cordate or sub-cordate at the base toothed along the entire margin, with 6-9 pairs of parallel veins, 3-8cm long by 2.5-3.5cm wide, pubescent on both sides though more so beneath. The petiole 10-15mm long. The fragrant white flowers borne in June in trusses 3-7cm long, each flower very small, often on short lateral branches. The fruit ovate, 8mm long, scarlet.

Viburnum cotinifolium **D Don** ❀ Prod. Fl. Nep. p.141 (1825)

syn. *V. polycarpum* Wall.
Introduced about 1830. A coarse, leggy plant, similar in foliage to *V. lantana* but distinguished by the shape of its flower-trusses.

A deciduous shrub from the Himalaya from Bhutan to Baluchistan growing to 3-4 metres by 4-5 metres spread. The leaves are ovate, oblong-ovate, elliptic to broadly elliptic, oval or round but never lanceolate, sharply pointed at the apex, rounded or heart-shaped at the base, entire or sinuately and finely toothed, with 6-8 pairs of prominent veins which are pubescent at first becoming glabrous as they age, 5-12cm long by 4-10cm wide, moderately pubescent above dull greyish-green or silvery-white and hairy beneath. The petiole up to 10mm long, widely winged and deeply grooved. The flowers borne in May-June all fertile, pink in bud opening to white or pinkish-white, widely funnel-shaped 4-7mm in diameter, in 5-rayed cymes 5-7cm across. The fruit ovate, 10mm long, red at first, turning black.

V. cotinifolium var. *lacei* **T R Dudley** From N Pakistan, N India near the Tibetan border and the Himalaya. Distinguished by its oblate-orbicular or spade-like (as in the suit of a pack of playing-cards) leaves up to 8cm long and 10cm wide, which are strongly retuse or truncate, rarely rounded at the apex and broad truncate to deeply cordate at the base as well as by the branchlets and corymbs which are largely glabrous.

V. cotinifolium var. *wallichii* **T R Dudley** From the Kingdom of Nepal. Markedly distinguished from the type by its much larger leaves that are usually very narrowly lanceolate, oblong-lanceolate or occasionally oblong-ovate, 15-25cm long and 4.5-9cm wide. The underside of the leaf is densely pubescent, and the flattened, narrow-winged petioles are only 10-15mm long. The inflorescences are smaller at 4-6cm wide by 3-4cm long, and the small congested flowers are 1-2mm in diameter. Overall the pubescence on all surfaces is between twice and four times as dense as the type.

In addition to the two varietas mentioned above many specimens intermediate between the two varietas and the type have been discovered in the regions of Northern India and Pakistan.

Viburnum cylindricum **Buch.-Ham. ex D Don** ❀ Prod. Fl. Nep. p.142 (1825)

syn. *V. coryaceum (V. coriaceum* Blume.) **Blume**
However, Kern disputes the synonomy pointing to the description of the plant from Nepal by D Don as having entire leaves, pubescent beneath, and tomentose cymes to justify maintaining *V. coriaceum* as a separate species. Introduced from India in 1881 and from China, by way of Paris, in 1896.

An evergreen shrub or tree from south-east Asia, Malaysia, Himalaya and China, growing normally to 4 metres but exceptionally to 10 metres. The leaves are extremely variable, oval, oblong or obovate, slender-pointed or rounded at the apex, wedge-shaped or rounded at the base. Generally entire in the Himalayan species, more often with a few indistinct teeth in the upper half of the leaf-blade in the Javanese and Sikkim species, with three or four pairs of veins arcuate-ascending and disappearing before reaching the margin, 8-20cm long by 4-10cm wide, quite glabrous, dark dull green above, paler beneath often bearded in the vein-axils. Upper surface covered with a waxy film which cracks and turns grey when rubbed or bent. The petiole 1.5-4cm long, light green or pinkish and slightly grooved. The flowers borne in July to September usually in flattened seven-rayed cymes branching three or four times, 8-15cm across on a short peduncle up to 2.5cm long composed of tubular, scented, white flowers up to 5mm long with lilac anthers. The fruit egg-shaped, 4-6mm long, black.

V. cylindricum var. *capitellata* **Wight & Arn.** The leaves are entire or sub-sinuate, the corolla glabrous (pilose in Wight's Icones), the drupe much compressed 8mm long but only 4mm wide.

V. cylindricum var. *longiflorum* **Kern** The tube of the corolla is about 6mm long compared with 3-4mm for the type.

Viburnum dasyanthum **Rehd.** ❀ Sargent, Trees and Shrubs ii.103 (1908)

Introduced by Wilson in 1907. The foliage is similar to *V. betulifolium* from which it is distinguished by the down on the corymbs and the outside of the corolla, the rounded base of the leaf and the more remote dentation. AM 1916.

A deciduous shrub from western and central China growing to 2-2.5 by 1.5-2 metres. The leaves are ovate to elliptic to oblong, slenderly pointed at the apex, rounded at the base. Remotely denticulate with 6-7 pairs of straight veins running out to the teeth, 6-12cm long by 2.5-3.5cm wide, dark green and glabrous above, paler and almost glabrous beneath except for a few hairs on the veins and in the vein-axils beneath, veins tinged red on the underside. The petiole purplish, slender, 15-20mm long with small stipules at the base. The flowers borne in June-July in open seven-rayed (occasionally five-) lax terminal corymbs 8-10cm across, with white flowers, the rays of the first order are glabrous whilst those of the second order are villous, flowering on the rays of the third or fourth order. The fruit ellipsoid, 8mm long, bright red.

Viburnum davidii **Franch.** ❀ Nouv. Archiv. Mus. Paris viii. 251 (1885)

Discovered by Armand David in Mupin, W Sichuan, in 1869, but only introduced by Wilson for Messrs Veitch in 1904. *V. davidii* is said to be dioecious, that is displaying staminate and pistillate flowers on different plants, and to require planting of male and female plants together to ensure fruiting. Whilst there is undoubted evidence that single plants are reluctant to set seed, this is more likely to be a consequence of the natural unwillingness of the genus as a whole to self-pollinate, rather than a more fundamental difference between one species and the whole of the rest of the genus. AM 1912, AGM (1969)1993.

A low-growing evergreen shrub from western China reaching 1.5 metres high with a spread of 2 metres or more. The leaves are narrowly oval or slightly obovate, tapered at the base more slenderly so at the apex. Strongly and conspicuously 3-veined, impressed above, elevated beneath, with the outer pair of veins emanating from the petiole and anastomosing before reaching the apex, often obscurely or shallowly toothed near the apex, 5-15cm long by 3-6cm wide, dark green above, pale below, glabrous on both surfaces except for small tufts of down on the vein-axils beneath. The petiole deep red, 5-20mm long. The flowers borne in June are dull white, 3mm wide densely crowded in stalked stiff cymes 5-8cm across. The fruit ovoid or globose-ovoid, 6mm long, bright blue.

V. davidii **'Angustifolium'** ❀ A cultivar with a narrower and shorter leaf than the type. Malecot considers that this may be a hybrid between *V. calvum* and *V. davidii*. There is a variegated form at the Oxford Botanic Garden.

Viburnum dentatum **L.** ❀ Sp. Pl. 268 (1753)

The arrowwood or southern arrowwood viburnum, so named because the American Indians used it to make arrows as the wood is heavy, very hard, and can take a high polish. Introduced to Britain from North America in about 1736.

Because *V. dentatum* is a polymorphic species, it suffers more than most of the genus from nomenclatural variations; because of the variability of the species, many of the named varieties are connected by intermediate forms. Through its adaptations to widely differing cultural conditions ranging from dry to wet soils, sand dunes to dense woodlands, temperature variations between the most extreme of the United States as well as a marked ability to interbreed, much confusion has arisen over whether there are distinct species or merely varietas or formas of but one species.

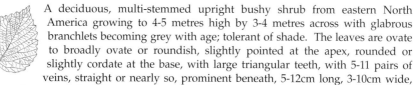 A deciduous, multi-stemmed upright bushy shrub from eastern North America growing to 4-5 metres high by 3-4 metres across with glabrous branchlets becoming grey with age; tolerant of shade. The leaves are ovate to broadly ovate or roundish, slightly pointed at the apex, rounded or slightly cordate at the base, with large triangular teeth, with 5-11 pairs of veins, straight or nearly so, prominent beneath, 5-12cm long, 3-10cm wide, pale green and glabrous above, sparsely downy beneath, turning reddish-brown in autumn. The petiole very thin, 8-12mm long, downy, sometimes with stipules. The flowers borne in May to July in slender-stalked cymes up to 12cm across, usually 5-7-rayed, all fertile white flowers 4mm in diameter. The anthers considerably longer than the corolla. The fruit roundish oval, 8-10mm long, blue-black, persisting well into the winter.

V. dentatum var. *canbyi* **(Rehd.) Blake** syn. *V. pubescens* var. *canbyi* **(Rehd.)Blake**
The leaves are thinner, larger and broader and with less pubescence beneath. The cymes are larger.

V. dentatum var. *deamii* **(Rehd.) Fernald** ❀ The leaves are almost perfectly circular with numerous sharp teeth, more or less pubescent beneath. The leaf stalk is distinctly hairy on the underside, the stipules are hairy and the shrub is more compact than the type.

V. dentatum **var. *indianense* Rehd.**   Similar to *V. dentatum* var. *deamii*, and indeed considered synonymous by some authors, but the leaf stalk is only pubescent on the upper side (in the groove) and the leaves are almost completely glabrous beneath. The leaf, although roughly circular, is not as perfectly circular as those of *V. dentatum* var. *deamii*, and the teeth are coarser.

V. dentatum **'Longifolium'** ❀ The leaves are longer then the type.

V. dentatum var. *lucidum* **Ait.**   The leaves are thin, ovate-lanceolate to rotund, sharply acute to short-acuminate at the apex, usually with between 10 and 20 teeth on each side. The petioles are glabrous, as is the lower leaf surface except for pubescence in the vein axils only. The common form in moist woods in the northern United States.

V. dentatum var. *pubescens* **Ait.** ❀ The downy arrowwood, not as hardy as the type and grows as a low straggling bush. The leaves are of a thicker texture and more downy on the branchlets and underside of the leaf.

V. dentatum var. *scabrellum* **Chapm.** ❀ Very similar to *V. dentatum* var. *dentatum*, the only difference being in the flowers where the calyx and corolla are densely hairy on the outside.

V. dentatum var. *venosum* **(Britton) Gleason** The leaves are thicker and more rounded than the type, often broader than they are long with a thick scurfy pubescence, especially beneath with prominent veins. The shrub is generally only 1.5-2 metres high and is probably not in cultivation.

V. dentatum **'Variegatum'** Mentioned since 1854 as a form with variegated leaves, but apparently no longer in cultivation.

V. dentatum **'White and Blue'** ❀ Named for the whiteness of the flowers and the bright blue fruit.

Three cultivars have been introduced by Synnestvedt Nurseries, Round Lake, Illinois:

V. dentatum **NORTHERN BURGUNDY®** **'Morton'** ❀ A shrub with a rounded habit growing to 2.5-3 metres high, with lustrous leaves turning burgundy in autumn.

V. dentatum **AUTUMN JAZZ®** **'Ralph Senior'** ❀ Growing to 4-5 metres high with a spread of 2.5-3 metres and of upright or vase-shaped habit. The leaves are glossy, turning red in autumn, and the petioles are red. Reputed to be more tolerant of wet soils.

V. dentatum **CHICAGO LUSTRE®** **'Synnestvedt'** A shrub 3-4 metres high by 2.5-3 metres wide of upright rounded habit with deep green foliage turning orange-red in autumn, usually later than other forms of *V. dentatum*.

Viburnum dilatatum **Thunb.** ❀ Fl. Jap. 124 (1784)

syn. *V. lantana* var. *japonicum* Fr. & Sav.
The linden viburnum, introduced by R Fortune in 1846. AM 1968.

A deciduous, upright, spreading shrub from China and Japan growing to 2.5-3 metres by 2-2.5 metres across. The leaves are broadly ovate, roundish or obovate, pointed and tapering at the apex, rounded or heart-shaped at the base, hairy on both sides, coarsely short-mucronate toothed with 5-8 pairs of veins, 5-10cm long, the same wide, bright green above, lighter beneath, hairy on both sides and with prominent red veins. The petiole 10-20cm long, red and hairy. The flowers borne in May-June are very numerous on hairy stalked cymes of pure white flowers, all fertile 6mm in diameter, mainly 5-rayed and 8-12cm across. The fruit roundish ovoid, up to 8mm long, bright red and remaining on the plant well into the winter as they are unpalatable to birds.

V. dilatatum **'Asian Beauty'** An upright growing selection with cherry-red fruit which retain their colour well into the winter.

V. dilatatum **'Catskill'** Introduced by the US National Arboretum in 1966 from a selection made in 1958 from plants raised from seeds from Japan, selected for its compact habit and distinguished by its smaller, rounder leaves and good autumn colour of yellow, orange and red. 'Catskill' grows to 2 metres high by 3 metres wide.

V. dilatatum **'Erie'** ❀ Introduced by the US National Arboretum in 1971, selected for the profusion, persistence and unusual colour of the fruits which ripen to red on top and orange beneath but turn, with the first frosts, to a coral-pink which intensifies with further frosts, the clusters persist well into the winter, long after the leaves have fallen.

V. dilatatum **f.** *hispidum* **Nakai.** ❀ The young branches, petioles and inflorescence are pubescent with spreading simple stiff hairs about 1mm long. The leaves and inflorescence are sparsely covered with fasciculate hairs but without conspicuous stellate hairs.

V. dilatatum **'Improved'** Selected in 1956 by John Vermeulen & Son, Neshanic Station, New Jersey, as more compact and more heavily berried than the type but by 1974 Vermeulen's were no longer listing this cultivar.

V. dilatatum **'Iroquois'** Introduced by the US National Arboretum in 1966. 'Iroquois' is the result of the cross between two selections of *V. dilatatum*. It forms a dense, rounded, fast-growing shrub, characterized by its large, heavy textured, dark green leaves which turn orange-red to maroon in autumn, abundant inflorescences of creamy white flowers, and larger, darker scarlet fruit.

V. dilatatum **'Michael Dodge'** A cultivar with yellow-orange fruit, growing to 2 metres.

V. dilatatum **'Moraine'** A fine fruiting selection.

V. dilatatum **f.** *nikoense* **(Hiyama) Hara** The leaves and petioles are sparsely hairy with spreading simple stiff hairs 0.5 to 1mm long, but lacking stellate hairs.

V. dilatatum **f.** *pilosum* **Nakai** The young branches, petioles and inflorescence are covered with conspicuous stellate hairs mixed with simple stiff hairs but without conspicuous spreading hairs.

V. dilatatum **'Sealing Wax'** ❀ Exhibited by Hillier & Sons at the RHS Great Autumn Show in September 1968, the fruit is a spectacular bright red.

V. dilatatum **'Xanthocarpum'** ❀ A yellow-fruited form which will not come true from seed. The foliage is a lighter green than the type and the fruit persists longer than any of the other yellow-fruited viburnum. AM 1936.

Viburnum (dilatatum x lobophyllum) 'Oneida' Egolf ✿ Baileya
14:115-7 (1966)

Introduced by the US National Arboretum 'Oneida' was selected for its abundance of flowers in May and sporadically throughout the summer, together with the persistence of its glossy dark red fruits.

A deciduous hybrid growing to 3-3.5 metres by 3 metres spread, the leaves are elliptic, elliptic-ovate or obovate, sharply pointed at the apex, broadly cuneate at the base, with 5-7 lateral veins on each side of the midrib running to coarse teeth, 6-12cm long, 4-8cm wide, dark green and slightly hairy above when young, becoming glabrous, lighter beneath with tufts of hairs on the midrib and in the vein-axils. The petiole 2-4cm long. The flowers borne in May in terminal cymes 10-14cm across, the fertile creamy-white flowers 4-5mm across. The fruit elliptic-ovate, 7-10mm long, red.

Viburnum edule (Michx) Raf. ✿ Med. Repos. N. York II.v.354 (1808)

Syn. *V. pauciflorum* Raf., *V. eradiatum* House
The squashberry or mooseberry. Generally found in woods and thickets but rarely cultivated, probably on account of the small flower trusses to which the specific epithet of its synonym refers. Introduced in 1880. Very hardy, having its origins as far north as Labrador and Alaska.

A deciduous straggling shrub from North America and Canada growing to 2 metres by the same across which thrives in moist and shady conditions. The leaves are nearly circular to broadly ovate, often with three short lobes at the apex, rounded or broadly truncate at the base, unevenly serrate, with 3 to 5 pairs of veins, 5-8cm long, the same wide, glabrous above, glabrous or slightly pubescent beneath. The petiole 10-25mm long, without stipules. The flowers borne in May-June up to 30 all fertile in small 5-rayed cymes 2-3cm across, each flower white, about 7mm in diameter. The fruit ellipsoid, 8mm long, red.

Viburnum erosum Thunb. Fl. Jap. 124 (1784)

Introduced by Fortune from China in 1844, later by Maries and Sargent from Japan. Possibly somewhat tender, plants growing on the slopes of Mount Fuji are found only in the prairie regions up to 900 metres. A very polymorphic species with more than a dozen formas and varietas, many associated with very small localities, described by different Japanese and Chinese botanists who singularly fail to agree on the taxonomy and which have not been included as their addition would be purely academic. There is a white-variegated form in cultivation in Japan.

A slender deciduous shrub of erect habit with much-forked branches, of somewhat straggly appearance growing to 1.5-2 metres high by 1-1.5 metres across from sunny hills and low elevations in the mountains of Japan, China and Korea. The leaves are oval-elliptical or obovate, pointed at the apex, wedge-shaped to rounded at the base, sharply toothed, with 7-10 vein-pairs, 4-8cm long by 3-5cm wide, glabrous or very sparingly pilose at first, becoming smooth and often lustrous above, glabrescent beneath except for hairs on the veins or stellate hairs in the lower part. The petiole very short, 2-5mm tomentose and with stout stipules. The flowers borne in May-June in loose 5-rayed cymes 5-8cm across, each fertile flower white, 4 mms in diameter with prominent stamens. The fruit globose or roundish-ovoid, 6mm long, red.

Viburnum erubescens **Wall.** ❀ Cat. nn. 459, 7464

A semi-evergreen shrub from Sri Lanka, India, Himalaya, N Burma and China growing to 3-5 metres by 2-4 metres across. The leaves are elliptic, elliptic-ovate or oblong, acuminate at the apex, cuneate to round at the base, neatly serrate along the whole of the edge of the leaf, downy or glabrous beneath, veins prominent beneath in 5-7 pairs, 5-10cm long by 2-5cm wide, dark and fairly glossy green above, lighter beneath with a distinctly reddish central vein. The petiole reddish, about 2.5cm long.The flowers borne in early June pink in bud opening white flushed with apricot-pink in long, loose, pendant panicles 7-10cm wide and 5cm long. The fruit ellipsoid, 6-5mm wide, green at first, turning red then black.

V. erubescens **var.** *carnosulum* **W W Smith** The leaves are more fleshy, not membranaceous, the apex and the base more cuneate, the veins more obscure, the peduncles shorter and the inflorescence more congested.

V. erubescens **var.** *gracilipes* **Rehd.** ❀ The flower panicles are larger than the type, 7-12cm long, whilst the leaves are more glabrous and rounded at the base. FCC 1988.

V. erubescens **var.** *limitaneum* **W W Smith** Differing from the type in the oval leaves, the apex more or less rounded and not acuminate or obtuse, the slender peduncle and with fewer flowers in the inflorescence.

Viburnum farreri **Stearn** ❀ Taxon xv.22 (1966)

syn. *V. fragrans* Bunge, not Loisel.

For a long time this species was referred to as *V. fragrans*, having been named by Alexander von Bunge in 1833. However the French doctor-botanist J L A Loiseleur-Deschamps had already published this name in about 1824 in his *Herbier General de l'Amateur* which was published in parts between 1814 and 1827. In his description he noted 'We do not know the country of origin of the pretty Viburnum; we have seen it at M. Noisette's (a nurseryman) who brought it from England five years ago as a new species.' Given the delay of five years one would have expected the new species to have been given a name already, and indeed it had been, the same species is clearly portrayed in the *Botanic Register* of 1820 at Plate 456 as *Viburnum odoratissimum*. What is inexplicable is how this oversight came about since Loiseleur appears to have been reasonably assiduous in his research and the *Botanic Register* was certainly available to him; did he have an overwhelming desire to name a new species or, given that the *Herbier* was a publication for amateurs was he less diligent in his research? To compound matters the new attribution was scarcely noticed at the time except by the eagle eye of the editor of the second edition of the *Herbier* which was published six years later, when it was given the correct name. Even Steudel in his *Nomenclature Botanicus* a decade later, failed to note the correction and instead coined the name *V. dubium* Steud. as taking precedence over *V. fragrans*, presumably as a warning to others as to the doubtful validity of either name.

Because the error had been rectified so soon it became easy for botanists to adopt von Bunge's name but they did not reckon with the growing authority of the International Code for Botanic Nomenclature and its rigorous insistence on striking out irresponsibly published names; the battle started in the 1930s but it was not until 1966 that Professor W T Stearn conceded defeat and published the new name of *V. farreri* in honour of Reginald Farrer who was so enchanted by the plant when he saw it growing in the wild in China in 1914; a description of his first encounter with the species is related in his book, *On the Eaves of the World*.

Although there are herbarium specimens dating from as early as 1835, it was only in 1911 that seed was collected by Purdom in the Minchow Temple Gardens in Gansu and propagated by Veitch. Purdom collected two forms, # 689 with white flowers and # 690 with pink flowers; it was not until 1920 that they first flowered. AM 1921, AGM (1923)1993.

A deciduous, strongly suckering shrub from China growing to 3 metres high with the same spread. The leaves are obovate or oval, acute at the apex, broadly cuneate to cuneate at the base, strongly toothed with 5-6 pairs of prominent parallel veins, 4-10cm long by 2.5-6cm wide, bronze when young, glabrous with tufts of down in the vein axils beneath, turning maroon in autumn before falling. The petiole 1-2cm long. The fragrant flowers are borne on the bare stems in winter from November to March in both terminal and lateral clusters 4-5cm across, each flower up to 1cm wide. Pink in bud opening white or with a hint of pink. The fruit oval, 5-8mm long, glossy scarlet turning black.

V. farreri '**Bowles' Variety**' Raised by the Slieve Donard Nursery in Ireland in the 1930s and said to be a much superior form, but now almost certainly lost.

V. farreri '**Candidissimum**' ❀ syn.*V. farreri* 'Album'. Less hardy and more subject to frost damage than the type with larger pure white inflorescences. The leaves are a lighter yellowish-green and do not colour in autumn. AM 1926.

V. farreri **'Farrer's Pink'** ❀ A form with pink flowers although it is doubtful if the true clone is still in existence.

V. farreri **'Fioretta'** ❀ A compact form with pink flowers.

V. farreri **'Mount Joni'** syn. 'Joni'. An early flowering form which often flowers again in the spring with an abundant display of blossom.

V. farreri **'Nanum'** ❀ syn. *V. farreri* 'Compactum' A compact form growing to not more than 1 metre. Not as free flowering as the type. AM 1937.

Viburnum foetidum **Wall.** ❀ Cat. n. 466; Pl. As. Rar. i.49

The specific epithet refers to the unpleasant smell of the leaves and stems shortly after they have been cut from the shrub; the smell is said to be so persistent that it can still be detected in herbarium specimens more than 100 years old. Originally introduced by Wilson in 1901, later seed was sent to Britain by Forrest. A very variable species with variations in the foliage on a single plant being quite noticeable, in particular the leaves of strong young shoots are often distinctly 3-lobed. AM 1934.

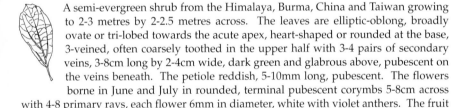 A semi-evergreen shrub from the Himalaya, Burma, China and Taiwan growing to 2-3 metres by 2-2.5 metres across. The leaves are elliptic-oblong, broadly ovate or tri-lobed towards the acute apex, heart-shaped or rounded at the base, 3-veined, often coarsely toothed in the upper half with 3-4 pairs of secondary veins, 3-8cm long by 2-4cm wide, dark green and glabrous above, pubescent on the veins beneath. The petiole reddish, 5-10mm long, pubescent. The flowers borne in June and July in rounded, terminal pubescent corymbs 5-8cm across with 4-8 primary rays, each flower 6mm in diameter, white with violet anthers. The fruit broadly oval to orbicular, 7mm long, scarlet-red sometimes spotted with cream.

V. foetidum **var.** *ceanothoides* **(C. H. Wright) Hand.-Mazz.** ❀ syn. *V. ceanothoides* C H Wright.
The leaves, obovate to elliptic-oblong, acute or rounded at the apex, cuneate at the base, are smaller at 2-5cm long, and the leaf stalk only 2-6mm long.

V. foetidum **var.** *integrifolium* **Kanehira & Hatushima** syn. *V. integrifolium* Hay
A small shrub with oblong to lanceolate leaves up to 9cm long but only 2.5cm wide without dentation, the inflorescences are almost glabrous and the flowers smaller at 3.5mm in diameter.

V. foetidum **f.** *rectangulatum* **Rehd.** ❀ syn. *V. rectangulatum* Graeb. The branches and branchlets have the characteristic of spreading nearly at right-angles and the leaves are smaller, 3-6cm long by 1.5-2cm wide.

Viburnum furcatum **Bl. ex Hook. f. & Thoms.** ❀ Journ. Linn. Soc. ii.175 (1858)
syn. *V. melanophyllum* Hayata
Introduced from Japan in 1892. Similar to *V. lantanoides* from which it is distinguished by its upright habit and less frequent branching, by the shorter stamens which are only half the length of the corolla and in the shape of the furrow in the seed. AM 1944, AGM 1993.

A large deciduous shrub from Japan and Taiwan growing normally to 2-3 metres but can reach 7 metres in its native habitat. The leaves broadly ovate to roundish with short, abrupt points and a heart-shaped base, the margins coarsely and irregularly toothed, with 7-10 pairs of parallel lateral veins, 10-20cm long and nearly as wide, dark green and downy at first becoming glabrous, the underside with stellate down on the midrib and veins, turning brilliant scarlet to reddish-purple in autumn. The petiole reddish, 3-6cm long. The fragrant white flowers borne in May-June are white, in stalkless cymes, two-leaved at the base, usually with five rays, 8-15cm across. The sterile marginal flowers up to 2.5cm in diameter, the central fertile ones much smaller. The stamens only about half the length of the corolla tube. The fruit broadly oval, 8mm long, red at first, turning purple-black when ripe.

V. furcatum **'Pink Parasol'** Described by Roy Lancaster in *The Garden* (July 1998) growing in Japan, but not yet available in Europe, the flowers remain a pale pink or pale to white at maturity.

Viburnum **x** *globosum* **Coombes** ❀ Plantsman 2(1):63-4 (1980)

V. davidii x *V. calvum*
A hybrid discovered by Ray Murphy at the West Hill Nursery of Messrs. Hillier, Winchester. Raised in 1964 from seed collected from *V. davidii* growing close to a specimen of *V. calvum*. It is intermediate between its parents, although its habit is more dense than either.

An evergreen hybrid shrub of rounded compact habit growing to 1-1.5 metres high. The leaves narrowly oval or slightly obovate approaching oblong, tapered at both ends, entire or with a few wide-spaced shallow teeth, one pair of veins starting near the base of the leaf and running to the margin at 1/2 to 2/3 of the length of the blade, together with a further 3-4 vein-pairs, 5-15cm long by 3-6cm wide, dark green above, pale below, the veins below almost white, glabrous on both surfaces except for small tufts of down in the vein-axils beneath. The petiole red when young, becoming paler, 6-20mm long, slightly grooved. The flowers borne in April-June dull white, densely crowded in stalked stiff cymes 5-8cm across. The fruit narrow oval, 6mm long, blue.

V. **x** *globosum* **'Jermyns Globe'** ❀ Selected by Messrs. Hillier as the best of the seedlings produced from the chance cross being of dense, rounded habit.

Viburnum wrightii 'Hessei'
(See p. 79)

Viburnum buddleifolium
(See p. 28)

Viburnum x *rhytidophylloides* 'Alleghany'
(See p. 67)

*Viburnum (*x *burkwoodii* x *carlesii)* 'Mohawk'
(See p. 30)

Viburnum sieboldii
(See p. 71)

Viburnum hupehense
(See p. 47)

Viburnum x *bodnantense*
(See p. 26)

Viburnum sargentii 'Onondaga'
(See p. 70)

Viburnum lantana
(See p. 50)

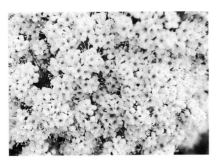

Viburnum rhytidophyllum
(See p. 68)

Viburnum x *rhytidocarpum*
(See p. 66)

Viburnum carlesii 'Charis'
(See p. 32)

Viburnum rhytidophyllum 'Roseum'
(See p. 68)

Viburnum utile
(See p. 78)

Viburnum x *carlcephalum*
(See p. 30)

Viburnum plicatum 'Mariesii'
(See p. 62)

*Viburnum (*x *carlcephalum* x *utile)*,
'Chesapeake' (See p. 31)

Viburnum x *burkwoodii* 'Anne Russell'
(See p. 29)

Viburnum bracteatum
(See p. 27)

Viburnum opulus 'Xanthocarpum'
(See p. 59)

Viburnum foetidum
(See p. 43)

Viburnum trilobum
(See p. 76)

Viburnum dentatum
(See p. 37)

Viburnum recognitum
(See p. 66)

Viburnum × *rhytidophylloides* 'Willowwood'
(See p. 67)

Viburnum cassinoides 'Nanum'
(See p. 33)

Viburnum rhytidophyllum 'Roseum'
(See p. 68)

Viburnum plicatum f. *tomentosum*
(See p. 62)

Viburnum utile
(See p. 78)

Viburnum x *juddii*
(See p. 49)

Viburnum plicatum f. *tomentosum* 'Shasta'
(See p. 63)

Viburnum macrocephalum
(See p. 54)

Viburnum carlesii 'Compactum'
(See p. 32)

Viburnum lantana 'Aureum'
(See p. 50)

Viburnum cinnamomifolium
(See p. 33)

Viburnum x *globosum* 'Jermyns Globe'
(See p. 44)

Viburnum davidii
(See p. 36)

Viburnum grandiflorum **Wall. ex DC.** ❀ Cat. n. 464

syn. *V. nervosum* sens. Hook. f. & Thoms., not D. Don
syn. *V. nervosum* Auct. not D. Don

Raised in England from seed collected by R E Cooper in 1914 in the forests of Bhutan above 11,000 feet. A valuable winter flowerer with a vivid red colouring to the leaf stalks and young stems in early summer. Closely related to *V. farreri* from which it is distinguished by its hairy, multi-veined leaves and larger flowers, the flowers have a strong aromatic scent. Young plants are distinctly upright-growing and do not flower as profusely. AM 1937.

A deciduous suckering shrub from the Himalaya to W China, growing to 2-3 metres by 1.5-2.5 metres across. The leaves are narrowly oval, elliptic-oblong to ovate, tapered towards both ends, pointed, finely and regularly toothed, with 6-10 veins in parallel pairs, 8-10cm long by 4-5cm wide, dullish green turning maroon, very pubescent beneath. The petiole reddish-purple, 2-2.5cm long. The flowers borne on the naked winter stems between January and March in dense cymes at the end of the preceding summer's growth, 5-7cm across, each flower with long corolla up to 12mm long and at least as much in diameter, carmine-red in bud, opening pink and lightening, though not fully white. Flowers are not as hardy as *V. farreri* and are likely to be damaged by frost. The fruit oval, 10-15mm long, red at first turning black.

V. grandiflorum **f.** *foetens* **(Decne.) N P Taylor & Zappi** ❀ syn. *V. foetens* Decne. More spreading in habit, distinguished by the leaves which are glabrous, or almost so, beneath, and the inflorescence which is also glabrous except at the nodes.

V. grandiflorum **f.** *foetens* **'Korean Form'** There is a plant of this name in the Royal Botanic Garden, Edinburgh which is said to be raised from seed collected in Korea in about 1934. Whilst it is undoubtedly a first-rate ornamental plant with larger and pinker flowers and trusses, the question remains as to how a species indigenous only to the Himalaya could have been collected in Korea.

V. grandiflorum **'Snow White'** Collected in Nepal by Col. D G Lowndes in 1950. The calyx is green, not red, and the corolla tube is white instead of pink. Certificate of Preliminary Commendation 1967, AM 1970, FCC 1974.

Viburnum harryanum **Rehd.** ❀ Mitteil. Deutsch. Dendrol. Ges. 263 (1913)

Quite distinct from any other of the cultivated viburnums in the rounded shape of its leaves which are often, particularly on strong shoots, borne in threes. Discovered by Wilson in western China in 1904 and named as a compliment to Sir Harry Veitch.

An evergreen shrub from western China growing to 2-2.5 metres high with the same spread. The leaves are orbicular to obovate or broadly ovate, tapered at the base, rounded at the apex except for a small mucro, margins entire or with a few obscure teeth, 1-2.5cm long, the same wide, dull dark green above, much lighter beneath, glabrous on both surfaces. The petiole very short, 2-3mm long, red. The flowers borne in June in a terminal umbel usually 7-rayed 3-4cm across composed of all perfect, pure white flowers 3mm in diameter. The fruit ovoid, pointed, 4mm long, bluish-black when ripe.

Viburnum henryi Hemsl. ❀ Journ. Linn. Soc. xxiii.353 (1888)

First reported by A Henry in 1887 from the Patung district in Hupeh and introduced into cultivation by Wilson in 1901 for J Veitch & Son. FCC 1910, AGM (1936)

An evergreen upright shrub or small tree with a somewhat stiff open-branched habit from central China growing to 2-3 metres high by 2-2.5 metres across. The leaves are narrowly oval, oblong or obovate, shortly pointed at the apex, wedge-shaped or rounded at the base, shallowly toothed, 4-12cm long by 2-5cm wide, dark shining green above, paler beneath, glabrous on both sides or with a little stellate down on the stalk and midrib. The petiole 1-2cm long, light green and slightly winged. The flowers borne in June-July white, about 6mm across all perfect and uniform in stiff pyramidical panicles 5-10cm wide at the base and the same length. The fruit oval, 8mm long, red turning black.

Viburnum x hillieri Stearn ❀ Journ. Roy. Hort. Soc. Lond. lxxxi.539 (1956)

A chance cross of *V. henryi* pollinated by *V. erubescens*. In 1950 seed from *V. henryi* was sown by Hillier who noticed that one of the seedlings was particularly vigorous and quite unlike its parent. With age it became clear that it was intermediate between *V. henryi* and *V. erubescens*, a plant of which had been growing next to the seed parent. *V. x hillieri* is a wide, spreading shrub, the leaves are broader and the habit more lax than *V. henryi*. The flowers have a tube longer than *V. henryi* but shorter than *V. erubescens*, the length of the stamens is also intermediate. To comply with the rules of nomenclature a Latin binomial diagnosis is required for its valid publication, however there was only one seedling raised by Hillier, namely *Viburnum x hillieri* 'Winton' ❀ AM 1956, AGM 1993.

An evergreen shrub of hybrid origin growing to 3-4 metres high by 2-3 metres across. The leaves are narrowly oval, oblong or obovate, shallowly toothed, 5-12cm long by 3-6cm wide, copper tinted when opening, shiny dark green above, paler beneath, turning bronze-red in winter. The petiole 2-3cm long, reddish on the upper side with more pronounced winging than *V. henryi*. The flowers borne in June-July in broad panicles of creamy-white flowers. The fruit oblong or obovate, 8-12mm long, red turning deep maroon to black.

Viburnum hupehense Rehd. ❀ Sargent, Trees and Shrubs ii.106 (1908)

Similar to *V. dilatatum*, from which it is distinguished by the stipules at the base of the leaf and the orbicular ovate leaves. Also similar to *V. betulifolium* which has glabrous, rhombic or oblong leaves. Discovered by Henry in 1888, but only introduced by Wilson as seed in 1908. AM 1952.

A deciduous shrub from Hupeh and Sichuan, China growing to 2-3 metres high by 1.5-2 metres across. The leaves are broad elliptic to roundish ovate, with a long point to the apex and truncate or slightly heart-shaped base, coarsely serrate with short acuminate, mucronate teeth and with with 6-8 vein-pairs, 5-7cm long by 3-5cm wide, dark green above, lighter beneath with denser hairs on the veins, pubescent on both sides, turning purplish-bronze in autumn. The petiole 15-20mm long, grooved and very hairy with persistent linear-lanceolate pubescent stipules. The flowers borne in May-June in terminal corymbs up to 5cm across of perfect white flowers usually 5-rayed, the peduncle 2cm long, densely fasciculate-pilose. The fruit ovate, 8-10mm long, orange-yellow turning red.

Viburnum ichangense Rehd. ❀ Sargent, Trees and Shrubs ii.105 (1908)

syn. *V. erosum* var. *ichangense* Hemsl., *V. erosum* var. *setchuense* Graeb.
Closely related to *V. erosum*, from which it is distinguished by the leaves which are smaller than *V. erosum* and more slender pointed. The flowers are less profuse and in smaller cymes, and the stamens shorter than corolla. Discovered in Hupeh by Henry, but not introduced until 1901 by Wilson.

A slender rather leggy-branched deciduous shrub from Hupeh, China growing to 1.5-3 metres high by 1.5-2.5 metres across. The leaves ovate or ovate-lanceolate, slender pointed at the apex, truncate or sub-cordate at the base, widely serrate with 6 to 9 pairs of straight veins, 3-6cm long by 1.2-3cm wide, yellowish-green above and covered with minute fasciculate or forked hairs, stellate-tomentose beneath beneath, particularly on the veins and with lax hairs on the mid-rib. The petiole 3-7mm long, pubescent, with persistent stipules at the base. The flowers borne in May-June are yellowish-white in small 4- or 5-rayed terminal or lateral pubescent corymbs 2-4cm across. The fruit ovoid, 6-7mm long, red and generally stellate-pubescent.

Viburnum x *jackii* **Rehd.** Journ. Arn. Arb. ii.125 (1920)

A horticultural hybrid of *V. lentago* x *V. prunifolium* which originated in the Arnold Arboretum before 1900 where it was noted by J G Jack in 1908. Intermediate between the parents, but closer to *V. lentago*; not of significant ornamental merit.

Viburnum japonicum **(Thunb.) Spreng.** ❀ Syst. i:934

syn. *Cornus japonica* Thunb., *V. buergeri* Miq., *V. macrophyllum* Bl., *V. japonicum* var. *boninsimense* Makino, *V. boninsimense* (Mak.) Koidzumi ex Nakai, *V. fusiforme* Nakai, *V. japonicum* var. *fusiforme* (Nak.) Massam
Introduced from Japan in about 1879 by C Maries. Not entirely hardy and preferably planted against a wall.

Not flowering in its early years but when established showing dense white-flowered umbels followed by clusters of brilliant red fruit although the latter are not always produced possibly because of the likely self-incompatibility.
Often confused with *V. odoratissimum* but differing in the flower and the leaf shape and veins which, in *V. japonicum*, run directly to the margin.

 A large evergreen shrub or small tree with with dark purple-brown branches from Kyushu, Japan and Taiwan growing to 1.5-2 metres with the same spread. The leaves are very variable, generally elliptic, ovate or broadly ovate, but sometimes roundish, oval or obovate, abruptly pointed or with a short, slender apex, slightly toothed or merely wavy in the upper half, the base tapering or rounded, with 5-8 pairs of parallel lateral veins, 8-15cm long by 4-10cm wide, strongly coriaceous, dark glossy green above, paler beneath with tiny dark glands on the areas between the veins. The petiole pale green 1.5-3cm long, without stipules, shallowly grooved above. The flowers borne in May-June uniformly perfect, white and very fragrant, up to 1cm in diameter in flattish, short stalked, usually seven-rayed cymes up to 6cm long by 8-12cm across, the peduncle about 15mm long branching 4 times. The fruit orbicular to elliptic, flattened, 8mm long, red.

Viburnum (japonicum x *dilatatum)* **'Chippewa' Egolf** ❀ Hort. Sci.

22:174-6 (1987)

Introduced by the US National Arboretum in 1987, at the same time as *V. (lobophyllum* x *japonicum)* 'Huron' which it resembles closely, the most noticeable difference being the duller leaf of 'Huron'.

A densely branched, semi-evergreen, multi-stemmed shrub of hybrid origin growing to 2.5-3.5 metres high by 3-4 metres across. The leaves are elliptic-obovate to ovate, entire in the lower half and finely serrate in the upper half, 6-11cm long, 4-7cm wide, though young plants may be larger up to 12-22cm x 6-15 cm, dark green above, lighter beneath turning dark maroon to bright red in autumn. The petiole 15-20mm long. The flowers borne in early May in cymes 10-18cm across each with 200-300 creamy-white flowers. The fruit oblong, 6-8mm diameter, dark red.

Viburnum x *juddii* **Rehd.** ❀ Journ. Arn. Arb. xvi.360 (1935)

The result of a cross between *V. bitchiuense* (pollinator) and *V. carlesii* made by William H Judd, propagator at the Arnold Arboretum in 1920. AGM (1960)1993.

A deciduous shrub of cultivated hybrid origin growing to 1-1.5 metres high with a similar spread. The leaves broadly ovate often with a slightly heart shaped base, pointed and irregularly toothed, 3-8cm long by 2-6cm wide, dull green above, greyish below, both surfaces soft with starry down. The petiole 6mm long. The fragrant pinkish-white flowers borne in April-May in a terminal rounded cluster 5-8cm across all fertile, each flower up to 8mm in diameter. The buds form in autumn and remain exposed throughout the winter. The fruit a flattened egg-shape, 6mm long, jet black.

Viburnum kansuense **Batal.** ❀ Act. Hort. Petrop. xiii.70 (1830)

Introduced from China by Wilson in 1908.

A deciduous shrub from western China growing to 2-3 metres high with the same spread. The leaves are broad ovate to roundish, with 3-5 deep lobes acute at the tips, cordate or rounded at the base coarsely toothed with 3-5 veins radiating from the top of the leaf stalk, 3-5cm long by 2-5cm wide, dark green and somewhat pubescent above, and with tufts of hairs in the vein-axils beneath, turning dull red in autumn.The petiole slender, 10-25mm long, with stipules. The flowers borne in May-June are in 5-7-rayed cymes up to 3cm across, all fertile pale pinkish-white, each flower 6mm in diameter. The fruit ellipsoid, 10mm long, red.

Viburnum koreanum **Nakai** ❀ Fl. Sylvat. Koreana xi.43 (1921)

A deciduous shrub from Korea growing to 2-3 metres high with the same spread. The leaves are obovate to roundish, acuminate at the apex, roundish or subcordate at the base, 3-lobed, the lobes 1-3cm long although often the young leaves are unlobed, coarsely dentate-serrate, 3-7cm long by 4-9cm wide, dark green and glabrous or with a few hairs near the margin, turning yellow or red in autumn before falling. The petiole 6-15mm long without glands but with stipules near the base. The flowers white, borne in May-June in terminal corymbs 2.5-4cm across with 5-30 normal flowers surrounded by enlarged sterile flowers. The fruit ellipsoid, 7-11mm long, green turning red when ripe.

Viburnum lantana L. ❀ Sp. Pl. 268 (1753)

The wayfaring tree, though mainly growing as a shrub in hedgerows, also, confusingly, known in America as the rowan tree, is one of the only two viburnums native to Britain. Vigorous, often used as a rootstock for grafting slower growing species. The fruit are said to be quite sweet to taste, but the flowers are somewhat unpleasant to smell, whilst the inner bark is acrid and both the fruit and bark have been used in medicine. *V. lantana* was long supposed to be a protection against witches and so was often planted close to houses and stables.

A deciduous shrub from Europe, North Africa, Asia Minor, Caucasus and N-W Iran growing to 3-4 metres high by 2-3 metres across. The leaves are broadly ovate or oblong, pointed or blunt at the apex, heart-shaped at the base, the upper surface velvety and the underside covered with a dense coat of starry down, minutely toothed, 5-12cm long by 3-10cm wide, light green. The petiole 1.5-3cm long. The creamy-white flowers borne in May-June in trusses 5-10cm wide composed of uniform flowers each 6mm across. The fruit oblong, 8mm long, red at first, turning black.

V. lantana '**Aureum**' ❀ Introduced by Spaeth of Berlin in 1921. The new growth and the young leaves are an attractive golden-yellow, keeping a tinge of yellow as they age, before becoming golden-yellow again before they fall.

V. lantana **var.** *discolor* **Huter** Leaves smaller and of a firmer texture, white tomentose beneath.

V. lantana '**Lanceolatum**' ❀ The leaves elongated.

V. lantana '**Macrophyllum**' ❀ Has larger, medium textured leaves and fruit clusters as much as 20cm across.

V. lantana '**Mohican**' ❀ Introduced by the US National Arboretum by D R Egolf in 1966 from a seedling selected in 1952 from seed collected in Poland. 'Mohican' has a dense, rounded form and grows to not more than 2 metres high and 2.5 metres wide. The leaf is a darker green and the fruit persists in the orange-red state for longer than the type.

V. lantana '**Rugosum**' The leaves are larger, darker green and more wrinkled, the cymes are larger and it fruits more abundantly.

V. lantana '**Variegatum**' ❀ The leaves variegated with yellow, awarded a Second Class Certificate in 1865.

V. lantana **'Versicolor'** ❀ Described in a French catalogue of 1913-14 as having leaves clear yellow in spring, golden yellow in summer and a wonderful shade in the autumn being a mixture of yellow, green, orange and violaceous red.

Viburnum lantanoides **Michx.** ❀ Fl. Bor. Am. i.179

syn. *V. alnifolium* Marsh

Introduced from North America in 1820. One of the fussier of the viburnums, *V. lantanoides* is much happier growing in moist shaded and lime-free conditions without competition from other trees or shrubs. Known as the hobblebush, witchhopple, trip-toe or shin-hopple viburnum, from the habit of its lower branches to bend and take root so as to trip passers by. Similar to *V. furcatum* and *V. sympodiale* from which it is distinguished by the longer stamens which are as long as the corolla tube, and stones with a Y-shaped groove on the ventral side. AM 1952.

A rather straggly deciduous shrub from eastern North America and Canada from Ontario to Quebec growing to 2-3 metres high with the same spread, although this can be greatly increased by its layering habit. The leaves broadly ovate to roundish in widely spaced pairs, the apex with a short point, the base heart-shaped, irregularly dentate, 10-20cm long, the same wide, dark green above, downy when young turning glabrous, lighter and more hairy beneath, especially on the veins and turning a brilliant claret-red in autumn. The petiole 3-6cm long. The flowers borne in May-June white in stalkless 5-rayed cymes 8-12cm across, the outer sterile flowers 20-25mm in diameter the central, fertile ones each 5-6mm in diameter. The fruit broadly oval, 8mm long, red at first turning black-purple when ripe.

V. lantanoides **'Praecox'** Flowering three weeks earlier than the type.

Viburnum lentago **L.** ❀ Sp. Pl. 268 (1753)

The sheepberry, nannyberry or wild raisin viburnum, introduced from North America in about 1761. A much branched, round topped large shrub or small tree which is sometimes used as a hedge in North America although it prefers a moist and shaded site. *V. lentago* can be confused with *V. prunifolium* and *V. rufidulum* but differs in the long taper-pointed leaves and winged petioles.

A deciduous shrub from eastern North America and Canada growing to 3-5 metres high by 2-4 metres across. The leaves are ovate to obovate, wedge shaped or rounded at the base, long and taper pointed at the apex, finely toothed, 5-10cm long by 3-5cm wide, dark shiny green above, lighter beneath glabrous except for short scurfy down on the veins, turning shades of yellow, orange and scarlet in autumn before falling. The petiole 15-25cm long, winged, often widening at the base and with an irregular wavy margin. The flowers borne in May-June are all perfect, creamy white in terminal stalkless cymes 8-12cm across, generally with 3-5 rays though sometimes as many as 7, each flower 6mm in diameter. The fruit oval, 12-15mm long, bright blue to blue-black with a whitish downy bloom.

V. lentago **'Nanum'** An uncommon shrub of spreading, bushy habit growing to 60cm high.

V. lentago **'Pink Beauty'** ❀ A form with pink berries turning more to violet.

V. lentago **'Show Girl'** A bud sport discovered in a forest in Massachusetts by Howard W Barnes, introduced in 1989. Dwarf in habit and with tri-colour variegation to the leaves depending on the season. No further information is available on this cultivar and it may have been withdrawn due to reversion which is common with many of the variegated viburnums.

V. lentago **f. *sphaerocarpum* Gray** Not significantly different from the type and inferior as an ornamental shrub, the fruit is subglobose rather than ellipsoid.

Viburnum lobophyllum **Graebn.** ❀ Engl. Jahrb. xxix.589

Closely related to *V. betulifolium* and *V. hupehense*. Introduced by Wilson in 1901. Brilliant red fruit and good autumn colour although the abundance of fruiting is only observed in mature plants. Despite the specific epithet the leaves are not lobed. AM 1947.

A deciduous shrub from central and western China growing to 3-5 metres by 3-4 metres across. The leaves broadly ovate to obovate, abruptly narrowed at the apex, rounded at the base and shallowly toothed with mucronate teeth, 5-6 pairs of veins, 5-11cm long by 4-8cm wide, bronze-green, glabrous except for a slight pubescence on the mid-rib above, lighter beneath with slightly pubescent veins beneath, turning claret before falling. The petiole 1-3cm long. The flowers borne in May-July in 7-rayed, long stalked cymes 7-10cm across, each flower perfect, white about 5mm in diameter, the flower stalks usually covered in a light brown stellate down. The fruit nearly globose, 8mm long, red.

Viburnum (lobophyllum x *japonicum)* **'Huron' Egolf** ❀ Hort. Sci.
22:174-6 (1987)

Introduced by the US National Arboretum in 1987, at the same time as *V. (japonicum* x *dilatatum)* 'Chippewa', which it resembles closely, the main difference being the duller leaf on 'Huron'.

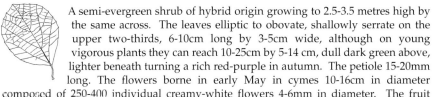

A semi-evergreen shrub of hybrid origin growing to 2.5-3.5 metres high by the same across. The leaves elliptic to obovate, shallowly serrate on the upper two-thirds, 6-10cm long by 3-5cm wide, although on young vigorous plants they can reach 10-25cm by 5-14 cm, dull dark green above, lighter beneath turning a rich red-purple in autumn. The petiole 15-20mm long. The flowers borne in early May in cymes 10-16cm in diameter composed of 250-400 individual creamy-white flowers 4-6mm in diameter. The fruit ovoid, 7-8mm in diameter, dark red.

Viburnum luzonicum **Rolfe** Journ. Linn. Soc. xxi.310 (1884)

syn. *V. villosifolium* Swartz
A very variable species where the indumentum and dentation of the leaf varies markedly with habitat. As a result many names have been proposed, with consequential complications in the nomenclature. The typical form comes from the Philippines where it is very common in thickets, secondary forests and waste places at low altitudes.

A deciduous shrub or small tree from the Philippines to S China, W China, Indo-China and Taiwan growing to 3-6 metres with a similar spread. The leaves are ovate to oblong or lanceolate, broad-acuminate or acute to obtuse at the apex, broadly cuneate to rounded or even slightly cordate at the base, the margin nearly entire to coarsely sinuate-dentate in the upper part, with 5-7 pairs of lateral veins straight ascending and usually ending in the marginal teeth, although the lower ones may anastomose before reaching the margin, 3-8cm long by 2-5cm wide, dark yellowish-green above, paler beneath, the young leaves usually densely pubescent with simple stellate hairs, particularly on the veins, becoming almost glabrous except for the midrib and the cilia of the margin. The petiole thin, 5-10mm long, densely pubescent and slightly channelled above, without stipules. The white flowers borne in April in terminal and axillary cymes 3-5cm across, branching two or three times, the axes densely ferrugineous pubescent, on a short peduncle up to 2cm long, with 3-6 slender primary rays about 1cm long, the flowers slightly fragrant, each one 3-5mm in diameter. The fruit globose, pubescent, 6-7mm long by 4-6mm diameter, red.

V. luzonicum **var.** *apoense* **Elmer** The leaves are sub-coriaceous, nearly glabrous except for the midrib on both sides, narrow, ovate-lanceolate, the apex long-acuminate, the margin nearly entire, only obscurely dentate and the primary veins often anastomosing.

V. luzonicum **var.** *floribundum* **(Merr.) Kern** syn. *V. floribundum* Merrill The leaves are chartaceous, nearly glabrous except for the midrib and the primary veins, ovate, the apex acute to short-acuminate, the margin rather strongly dentate, especially in the upper half, the primary veins for the greater part terminating in the teeth.

V. luzonicum **var.** *formosanum* **(Hance) Rehd.** Found in Taiwan and China, has larger, wider and more dentate leaves with less pubescence.

V. luzonicum f. *matsudai* **Hayata**   syn. *V. matsudai* Hayata   A form with more pointed leaves.

V. luzonicum var. *oblongum* **Kaneh. & Sasak.** ❀ The leaves are more oblong.

V. luzonicum var. *sinuatum* **(Merr.) Kern**   syn. *V. sinuatum* Merrill   The leaves oblong-ovate, the apex slenderly acuminate, the margin coarsely sinuate-dentate, otherwise similar to *V. luzonicum* var. *floribundum*.

Viburnum macrocephalum **Fort.** ❀ Journ. Hort. Soc. ii.244 (1847)

syn. *V. macrocephalum* f. *sterile* Dipp.
Introduced by R Fortune from China in 1844, a tender shrub which requires a sheltered spot, preferably against a wall.   This is the largest of the 'snowball' viburnums; the wild form from China, *V. macrocephalum* f. *keteleeri* reproduces true from seed whilst the more showy garden form, *V. macrocephalum* f. *macrocephalum*, is sterile. AM 1927.

A deciduous or partly evergreen shrub from Chinese cultivation growing to 3-4 metres high by 2-3 metres wide. The leaves ovate, occasionally oval or oblong, rounded at the base, rounded or pointed at the apex, denticulate, 5-10cm long by 3-6cm wide, dull green with scattered hairs above, stellate down beneath. The petiole 1-2cm long. The flowers borne in May in large globular trusses up to 15cm in diameter of all sterile flowers each up to 4cm wide, apple-green at first opening to pure white.

V. macrocephalum f. *keteleeri* **(Carr.) Rehd.** ❀ Introduced from China about 1860. The wild form of *V. macrocephalum* with flat inflorescences up to 15cm across of perfect flowers surrounded by large sterile flowers.

Viburnum molle **Michx.** ❀ Fl. Bor. Am. i:180

syn. *V. demetrionis* Deane & Robins.
The Kentucky viburnum is a dense, bushy shrub with a purplish-grey peeling bark which reveals a shiny under-surface, tolerant of calcareous soils.   The specific epithet refers to the soft under-surface of the leaf.

A deciduous shrub from the central and southern states of North America growing to 3-4 metres high with a spread of 2-3 metres. The leaves are broadly ovate to roundish, slenderly pointed at the apex, deeply cordate at the base, coarsely toothed, with 8-10 pairs of veins, 6-12cm long by 4-10cm wide, dark green and glabrous or slightly pilose above, lighter and thinly pubescent beneath, especially on the veins. The petiole is slender and glabrous, 1.5-3cm long, generally one-third the length of the leaf blade, with small, early-deciduous, linear filiform stipules. The flowers borne in June are all perfect, white, in long-stalked cymes 5-8cm across, usually 5-7-rayed, each flower 6mm in diameter. The fruits are flat-ellipsoid, 8-10mm long, blue-black.

***V. molle* f. *leiophyllum* Rehd.** The underside of the leaf is glabrous apart from pubescence on the primary veins only.

Viburnum mongolicum (Pall.) Rehd. ✿ Sargent, Trees and Shrubs ii:111 (1908)

syn. *V. davuricum* Pall. A species rare in cultivation and rarely properly identified; chiefly of botanical interest. A shrub with spreading branches, the young branchlets stellate-pubescent becoming glabrous and yellowish grey in the second year.

A deciduous shrub from eastern Siberia and Inner Mongolia growing to 1.5-2 metres high with the same spread. The leaves are broad ovate, acute or rounded at the apex, rounded at the base, shallowly dentate, 3-6cm long by 2.5-4cm wide, densely stellate pubescent beneath. The petiole 5-8mm long. The flowers borne in May in small cymes 2-4cm across with only a few flowers 6-7mm in diameter, the white flowers mostly on rays of the first order. The fruit ellipsoid, 5-6mm long, red at first, turning black.

Viburnum mullaha Buch.-Ham. ex D Don ✿ Prod. Fl. Nep. 141 (1825)

syn. *V. stellulatum* Wall.

A tall deciduous shrub from the Himalaya from Kashmir eastwards and S-E Asia growing to 3-5 metres by 2-4 metres across. The leaves ovate to roundish-oval, long acuminate at the apex, rounded or broadly tapered at the base. Deeply but sparsely dentate in the upper half. 6-9 pairs of veins, tufts of hairs in the vein-axils, 7-15cm long by 5-8cm wide, mid-green and glabrous above, slightly lighter and stellate-pubescent beneath. The petiole 15-25mm long. The flowers borne in April-July in 5- or 6-branched large cymes of all perfect flowers in up to 7cm across, each flower white, 4-6mm in diameter. The fruit egg-shaped, 8mm long, yellow at first, turning red, slightly hairy.

***V. mullaha* var.*glabrescens* (C B Clarke) Kitam.** syn. *V. involucratum* Hook. f. & Thoms. (not Wall.) The corymbs have only a few scattered hairs and the leaves are glabrescent except on the veins beneath.

Viburnum nervosum D Don ✿ Prod. Fl. Nep. 141 (1825)

syn. *V. cordifolium* Wall. ex DC.

A loosely branching deciduous shrub from W China, Himalaya (Kumam to Bhutan),

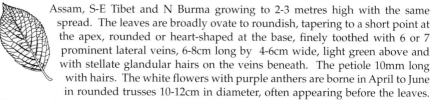

Assam, S-E Tibet and N Burma growing to 2-3 metres high with the same spread. The leaves are broadly ovate to roundish, tapering to a short point at the apex, rounded or heart-shaped at the base, finely toothed with 6 or 7 prominent lateral veins, 6-8cm long by 4-6cm wide, light green above and with stellate glandular hairs on the veins beneath. The petiole 10mm long with hairs. The white flowers with purple anthers are borne in April to June in rounded trusses 10-12cm in diameter, often appearing before the leaves. The fruit ellipsoidal, 6-8mm long, red at first turning black.

Viburnum nudum **L.** ❀ Sp. Pl. 268 (1753)

syn. *V. laevigatum* Willd. not Ait. The possumhaw viburnum, similar to *V. cassinoides.*

An irregularly branched deciduous shrub or small tree from E North America growing to 3-4 metres high by 2-3 metres wide. The leaves are oblong to elliptic or oval, acute, obtuse, rounded or abruptly pointed at the apex, rounded or cuneate at the base, margin entire or finely and irregularly toothed, 8-15cm long by 3-6cm wide, leathery, olive to dark glossy green and glabrous above, lighter beneath, with pinkish veins and purplish margins, turning dark red in autumn. The petiole 6-10 mm, narrowly winged. The flowers borne in June-July are yellowish-white, all perfect in long-stalked cymes 5-10cm across, each flower 5mm in diameter. The fruit oval, 8mm long, pink at first, turning blue-black.

V. nudum **var.** *angustifolium* **Torrey & Gray** Narrow elliptic leaves less than 5cm long and 12mm wide and of firmer texture.

V. nudum **'Pink Beauty'** ❀ The fruit are rose-pink, but turn black with the first frost.

V. nudum **'Winterthur'** ❀ A compact form with superior wine-red foliage in autumn, selected at the Winterthur Gardens, Delaware.

Viburnum obovatum **Walt.** Fl. Carol. 116 (1860)

syn. *V. laevigatum* Ait., *V. lanceolatum* Hill.

Commonly known as the small viburnum on account of the size of the leaves. A bushy low-growing shrub with thin grey branches and somewhat leathery leaves turning bright red in autumn.

A deciduous shrub from the eastern United States, South Carolina, Georgia and Florida growing to 1-2 metres with the same spread. The leaves are obovate, acute at the apex and at the base, entire or with a few small teeth in the lower half, 1.5-4cm long by 1-2cm wide, glossy dark green above, paler beneath. The petiole short, 4-6mm long. The flowers borne in June-July in small convex cymes 5-8cm across, barely showing above the leaves, each flower white 8mm in diameter. The fruit ovate, 6-8mm long, black.

Viburnum odoratissimum **Ker-Gawler** ❀ Bot. Reg. t.456

syn. *V. hasseltii* Miq., *V. arboricolum* Hayata, though whilst Kanehira treats *V. arboricolum* as a distinct species, Kern argues that the differences can be explained by the polymorphism of the species. In addition Kern argues that *V. liukiuense* Nakai, and *V. zambalense* Elmer are also synonymous with *V. odoratissimum*.

Quite tender, the current season's growth can be damaged by frost in a severe winter. *V. odoratissimum* is sometimes epiphytic. Specimens from the different regions of S-E Asia where this species grows have shown considerable differences, mainly in the shape and dimensions of the corolla.

An evergreen shrub or small tree from N-E India, S-E Asia, Japan, Taiwan, Java, Philippines and Celebes growing to 3-8 (sometimes 20) metres high by 3-5 metres wide. The leaves are elliptic, oval or obovate, shortly and bluntly acuminate at the apex, rarely rounded or even emarginate, wedge shaped and gradually tapering into the petiole at the base, entire or sparingly sinuate-dentate or with a few obscure teeth in the upper half of the leaf blade, with 5-7 pairs of primary veins at an angle of about 60° to the midrib, arcuately ascending, evanescent and indistinctly anastomosing near the margin, the midrib raised on both surfaces, 8-20cm long by 4-10cm wide, glossy green and glabrous above, paler and glabrous beneath except for a few scattered stellate hairs and tufts of down in the vein-axils. The petiole stout, 1.5-3cm long, grooved above. The flowers borne in May are pure or creamy white, 6mm wide and very fragrant, all perfect in terminal broadly pyramidical panicles 8-15cm high, 6-12cm wide at the base, branching three times. The fruit ovoid to ellipsoid, 6-7mm long by 4-5mm wide, green at first, turning red finally purplish-black.

V. odoratissimum **var.** *conspersum* **W W Smith** Differing from the type in the branchlets and inflorescences which are sparsely stellate-pubescent, the leaves are oval and generally rounded at the apex and, when young, have a sparse fulvous stellate-pubescence on the midrib, the petiole at first has a dense stellate-pubescence soon becoming glabrous.

V. odoratissimum **'Emerald Lustre'** ❀ A selected form with lustrous green leaves and young shoots tinged with pink.

V. odoratissimum **var.** *serratim* **Makino** This was described as a cultivated plant showing depressed serrate leaves and a similar form is also found in wild populations, but Hara does not consider it to be worthy of a separate taxon.

V. odoratissimum '**Variegatum**' A variegated variety with leaves mottled with white and pink, often grown as a pot plant in Japan.

Viburnum opulus **L.** ❀ Sp. Pl. 268 (1753)

The guelder rose or, to the Americans, the European cranberry bush, cultivated since antiquity throughout Europe.
The Asiatic race distribution in temperate eastern Asia is geographically isolated from the typical *V. opulus* of Europe, but is so similar in many characteristics that it can be regarded as a geographical variety of *V. opulus*.

A deciduous suckering shrub from Europe, including th British Isles, N-W Africa, Asia Minor, the Caucasus and parts of Central Asia growing to 3-5 metres high by 3-4 metres across. The leaves nearly orbicular, deeply three-lobed, though sometimes with 4 or 5 lobes, the base truncate, the lobes pointed, coarsely and irregularly toothed, 5-10cm long, the same or more wide, dark green and glabrous above, lighter and downy beneath especially on the veins, turning a brilliant wine-red in autumn. The petiole 1-2cm long with two thin linear, attenuate-tipped stipules at the base and between 1 and 6 large concave-topped, sessile or sub-sessile glands near the junction with the leaf blade. The flowers borne in May-June in cymes 5-8cm across with a border of showy sterile white flowers each up to 2cm in diameter surrounding the central fertile flowers which are much smaller at 6-8mm in diameter. The fruit globose, 10-15mm long, 8mm wide, bright red.

V. opulus '**Aureum**' ❀ The young leaves start bronze, becoming yellowish-green and lightening, before turning darker green in the autumn. In full sun the yellow leaves may become green prematurely.

V. opulus var. *calvescens* (**Rehd.**) **Hara** ❀ syn. *V. sargentii* var. *calvescens* Rehd. Variable in the degree of hairyness, typically having almost glabrous leaves, petioles, branches and peduncles. The leaf stalk is longer at 3-4cm and the anthers are dark purple.

V. opulus var. *calvescens* f. *flavum* (**Rehd**) **Hara** A form with yellow anthers and drupes, the leaves are pubescent beneath. Very rare, from Japan and China.

V. opulus '**Compactum**' ❀ A dwarf form, said to be an old Dutch cultivar from before 1940, with smaller leaves and a dense habit which is particularly suitable as a hedge, growing to no more than 1.5 metres high with a similar spread which flowers and fruits reliably. AM 1962, AGM (1964)1993.

V. opulus '**Fructu-Luteo**' ❀ Known in cultivation from as early as 1901 a form with bright yellow fruits tinged pink at first, maturing to a deeper chrome-yellow and becoming translucent with the first frosts.

V. opulus f. *hydrangeoides* **H Hara**   syn. *V. opulus* var. *calvescens* f. *hydrangeoides* (Nakai) Hara   A form with all sterile flowers in subglobose, somewhat loose inflorescences up to 14cm in diameter.   Found in gardens in Hokkaido.

V. opulus **'Nanum'** ❀ Originated in France about 1841.   A small shrub of dense tufted habit growing to less than 1 metre high, the leaves not more than 4cm long.   It flowers reluctantly.

V. opulus **'Notcutt's Variety'** ❀ More freely flowering with larger flowers, more deeply lobed leaves, larger fruit and better autumn colour. Possibly a cross between *V. opulus* and *V. trilobum*. AM 1930, AGM (1984)1993.

V. opulus **'Park Harvest'** ❀ A large-growing cultivar with leaves bright yellow above, darker beneath.

V. opulus f. *puberulum* **(Komarov) Sugimoto**   A form with pubescent leaves with spreading hairs on the underside and also often hairy on the branches, petioles and peduncles.

V. opulus **'Roseum'** **('Sterile')** ❀ The snowball tree.   Probably the oldest known garden viburnum recorded in the 16th century as "Sambucus Rose" or rose elder. Although the common name 'guelder rose' is now used for all *V. opulus*, it was originally reserved for *V. opulus* 'Roseum', referring to its origins in Gelderland, Netherlands. The flowers are double and in large globose cymes starting greenish-white in bud before opening to creamy-white snowballs up to 6cm in diameter.   As all the flowers are sterile the possibility of any fruit is lost, however the good autumn colour is retained.   AGM (1964)1993.

V. opulus **'Tatteri'**   Reputed to have attractive white variegated leaves and double flowers, but very doubtful that it is still in cultivation.

V. opulus **'Ukraine'**   Selected in the Kiev Botanic Gardens for its productivity and large superior quality fruit.   Reaches fruiting age 1-2 years after planting (from Nursery).

V. opulus **'Variegatum'**   A form with variegated leaves.

V. opulus **'Xanthocarpum'** ❀ Introduced by Spaeth's Nursery in Berlin in 1910. The yellow-fruited European cranberry bush.   A compact, round-headed shrub with yellow fruit becoming a translucent golden yellow particularly after the first frosts. The berries persist well if they are not taken by birds.   There can be confusion between this and *V. opulus* 'Fructu-Luteo'. *V. opulus* 'Xanthocarpum' is distinguished by the fruit which are always yellow, starting as a shiny apricot-yellow, whereas those of *V. opulus* 'Fructu-Luteo' are pink at first.   AM 1932, FCC 1966, AGM (1969)1993.

Viburnum phlebotrichum **Sieb. & Zucc.** Abh. Akad. Muench. iv.III.173 (1846)

syn. *V. phlebotrichum* var. *latifolium* Nakai, *V. phlebotrichum* f. *latifolium* (Nakai) Sugimoto
Similar to *V. setigerum* which is distinguished by its larger and longer-stalked leaves, whilst *V. phlebotrichum* is a smaller slender shrub with smooth yellow-grey branches, generally glabrous or with a thin pubescence when young.

A deciduous shrub from the mountains of Japan growing to 2-2.5 metres with the same spread. The leaves are narrowly ovate-oblong, pointed at the apex, obtuse or tapered at the base, regularly triangular dentate with 6-9 vein-pairs, 3-8cm long by 2.5-4cm wide, glabrous above, silky pubescent beneath, turning crimson in autumn. The petiole 15 mm long, usually glabrous. The flowers borne in May-June in pendulous cymes 2-4cm across with only a few rather small pendulous white or pinkish flowers. The fruit broadly ovoid, 8-10mm long, red.

V. phlebotrichum f. laciniatum F. Maekawa ex Toyama An abnormal form with incised leaves found on Mt. Unzen of Kyushu by S Toyama in July 1931.

V. phlebotrichum f. xanthocarpum Hayashi A yellow-fruited form.

Viburnum plicatum **Thunb.** ❀ Trans. Linn. Soc. ii.332 (1794)

V. plicatum is unique amongst the viburnums in its horizontal habit, when well grown the pyramid-shaped structure is outstanding when covered with blossom. This is enhanced by the habit of self-layering which will allow the shrub to expand horizontally to any size.

The problems of nomenclature are well illustrated by discussion of *V. plicatum* and *V. tomentosum*. Two forms are described by the Swedish botanist Carl Pehr Thunberg as *V. tomentosum*, the wild (fertile) form, and *V. plicatum* the cultivated (sterile) form found in Japanese gardens at the time. As the name *V. tomentosum* had precedence, *V. plicatum* was considered to be a variety of *V. tomentosum*.

However in 1945 Dr Alfred Rehder of the Arnold Arboretum pointed out that the name *V. tomentosum* had already been used by Jean Baptiste de Lamark, a French botanist, in 1778 to describe *V. lantana*, despite the fact that this had already been classified as *V. lantana* by Linnaeus. Thus, although the name *V. tomentosum* which Thunberg had described in 1784, was not confusing in any way, the rules had to be strictly applied and the name declared invalid. As a consequence the name *V. plicatum* became the name for the species as a whole, whilst the wild form was reduced to the status of a forma of the species, namely *V. plicatum* f. *tomentosum*.

So, whilst *V. plicatum* is the correct name for the species as a whole, individual plants belong either to *V. plicatum* f. *plicatum* (the snowball forms) or to *V. plicatum* f. *tomentosum* (the wild fertile forms), but for the sake of brevity many nurserymen fail to make the distinction between the two forms, preferring to label all the cultivars as *V. plicatum* only.

Viburnum plicatum f. *plicatum* Thunb. ❀

Introduced by R Fortune from China in 1844, although it was known to be growing in Japanese and Chinese gardens as early as 1712 when it was first mentioned by Kaempfer. FCC 1893, AGM (1969)

A deciduous spreading shrub from Japan and China growing to 2-3 metres high by 4-5 metres or more across. The leaves broad-ovate to elliptic-obovate, shortly pointed at the apex, rounded or wedge-shaped at the base, serrate in the upper part, 4-10cm long by 3-6cm wide, dark green above, lighter beneath with hairs particularly on the veins and in the vein-axils, turning dark red to brown in the autumn. The petiole 15-20mm long. The white flowers borne in May-June in rounded trusses up to 8cm or more in diameter composed of all sterile flowers, each flower 20-30mm across.

V. plicatum f. *plicatum* **'Chyverton'** Propagated by Nigel Holman in 1964 from a plant in the garden of Lionel Fortescue in Devon where it was growing to only 4 feet high but with a spread of 20 feet. AM 1965.

V. plicatum f. *plicatum* **'Grandiflorum'** ❀ A cultivar dating from 1914 or earlier with larger flower trusses and a more tiered habit than the type, the flowers are flushed pink or with a hint of apricot. AM 1961, AGM (1969)1993.

V. plicatum f. *plicatum* **'Mary Milton'** ❀ An upright, less vigorous pink-flowered form.

V. plicatum f. *plicatum* **'Rosace'** ❀ syn. 'Kern's Pink', 'Roseace'. A bud sport selected in 1957 by Carl Kern at the Wyoming Nursery, Ohio. The flowers are a distinct but delicate pink and the young leaves are distinctly bronze tinted. The whole shrub is smaller and more delicate than the type and parts of a branch, twig or flower can revert to the typical white form.

V. plicatum f. *plicatum* **'Rotundifolium'** ❀ Very similar to 'Grandiflorum', but with more rounded leaves.

Viburnum plicatum f. *tomentosum* (Thunb.) Rehd. ❀

Known in America as the double-file viburnum from the abundance of parallel rows of inflorescences with a profusion of creamy-white 'lace-cap' flowers in the spring. Introduced later than *V. plicatum* f. *plicatum* in about 1865. AGM (1969)

Similar to *V. plicatum* f. *plicatum* except for the flowers which are generally borne two to three weeks earlier in flattened trusses up to 10cm in diameter composed of a central section of small fertile surrounded by a single row of larger sterile flowers, each of these up to 25mm in diameter. The fruit are roundish to egg-shaped, 8mm long, coral red at first, turning blue-black when ripe.

V. plicatum f. *tomentosum* 'Cascade' ❀ A seedling from *V. plicatum* f. *tomentosum* 'Rowallane' selected in 1971 in Holland by Jac Shoemaker as an improved 'Mariesii', the abundance of large flowers give the effect of a snow-laden bush and the fruit are very prolific.

V. plicatum f. *tomentosum* 'Dart's Red Robin' ❀ A recent selection from Holland growing to less than 2 metres high, with profuse red berries in the autumn.

V. plicatum f. *tomentosum* 'Igloo' Selected at the Winterthur Gardens, Delaware in 1991, growing to 2 metres high with even greater spread, a profusion of snow-white, flat, lace-cap flowers in April forming a mound that resembles an igloo.

V. plicatum f. *tomentosum* 'Lanarth' ❀ Raised as a seedling by Mr P D Williams of Lanarth, Cornwall before 1930. Very similar to 'Mariesii' but the outer ray flowers are up to 50mm in diameter and the common stalk of the inflorescence is thicker and 12mm longer. It is likely that, due to the difficulties of differentiation, many plants of 'Lanarth' are sold as 'Mariesii' and vice versa; it is equally likely that many are neither but are in fact inferior seedlings. AM 1930, AGM (1969)

V. plicatum f. *tomentosum* 'Lanceatum' syn. *V. tomentosum* var. *lanceatum* Rehd. The leaves are narrower, lanceolate and more gradually acuminate, more pubescent beneath and the inflorescences are smaller with fewer fertile flowers.

V. plicatum f. *tomentosum* 'Mariesii' ❀ Introduced by Maries from Japan in 1877-9 for Messrs Veitch. Probably the best known of the cultivars of *V. plicatum*, 'Mariesii' has larger flower trusses, and the large, sterile, flowers can reach over 40mm in diameter. The leaves always have a more yellowish tint in the summer. Although it flowers prolifically, it rarely sets seed. AGM (1929)1993.

V. plicatum f. *tomentosum* 'Mariesii Snowfall' A seedling from 'Mariesii' exhibited by Collingwood Ingram in May 1965. AM 1965.

V. plicatum f. *tomentosum* 'Nanum Semperflorens' ❀ syn. *V. plicatum* f. *tomentosum* 'Watanabe'. A dwarf cultivar of dense habit with horizontal branches and small pure white flowers throughout the summer from June to October. Once established the flowering season tends to revert to the more normal months, but the summer flowering can be encouraged by early spring pruning. Distinguished from *V. p.* 'Summer Snowflake' by the habit which is not typically tiered. It is said that it was discovered by Mr Kenji Watanabe in the foothills of Mount Fuji near the town of Gotemba and propagated in his nursery in the mid-1950s.

V. plicatum f. *tomentosum* **'Newzam'** ❀ = *V. plicatum* f. *tomentosum* NEWPORT®. A dwarf and very compact form whose flowers are borne upright in large snowball-like clusters..

V. plicatum f. *tomentosum* **'Pink Beauty'** ❀ The sterile flowers are flushed with pink on opening, darkening to a deeper pink as they age; the leaves are tinged with bronze. Certificate of Preliminary Commendation 1969, AGM 1993.

V. plicatum f. *tomentosum* **'Roseum'** ❀ Raised at the Brooklyn Botanic Garden in the United States, 'Roseum' is not as hardy as the type. The flowers are creamy-white tinged with soft pink, deepening in colour as they age; they are a stronger pink if the soil is slightly acid and the climate cool.

V. plicatum f. *tomentosum* **'Rowallane'** ❀ Raised at the Rowallane Gardens, Saintfield, N Ireland. Slow-growing neat and compact shrub, rarely growing to more than 2 metres high and with smaller leaves and flower trusses than 'Lanarth' or 'Mariesii'; it is more likely to set seed than these. AM 1942, FCC 1956, AGM (1969)1993.

V. plicatum f. *tomentosum* **'Shasta'** ❀ Introduced by the US National Arboretum in 1979 as a cross between a selected *V. plicatum* f. *tomentosum* and *V. plicatum* f. *tomentosum* 'Mariesii'. The flowers are one and a half times the size of those of other cultivars and often have between 5 and 15 sterile florets dispersed within the central fertile flowers. Whilst the outer, sterile flowers of the type tend to be creamy, those of 'Shasta' are pure white. AM 1988.

V. plicatum f. *tomentosum* **'Shoshoni'** ❀ Introduced by the US National Arboretum in 1987, 'Shoshoni' is a dwarf form growing to just 1.2 metres high and 2.4 metres wide in 17 years. It was selected for its suitability in smaller gardens, whilst retaining the flower and leaf colouring characteristics of the type. It was produced as a result of controlled pollination of 'Shasta' in 1967 when seven seedlings were noted with greatly reduced internodal length, smaller leaves and thinner branches than the parent. Of these only one produced abundant flower trusses, albeit smaller than the parent, together with long-persisting red fruit.

V. plicatum f. *tomentosum* **'St. Keverne'** ❀ Raised at St. Keverne, Cornwall.

V. plicatum f. *tomentosum* **'Summer Snowflake'** ❀ syn. 'Fujisanensis', 'Mt. Fuji'. A Canadian cultivar with a prolonged flowering period, similar to 'Nanum Semperflorens' for which it is often mistaken, the leaves are darker, more leathery and more persistent than 'Nanum Semperflorens' and with age the shrub develops the typical tiered habit.

V. plicatum f. *tomentosum* 'Triumph'   A selection from *V. plicatum* f. *tomentosum* 'Newzam' with a dense compact, almost perfectly round form, strong, vigorous growth and exceptionally heavy blooming.

V. plicatum f. tomentosum 'White Delight'   A very dense, upright plant, not spreading as wide as *V. plicatum* f. *tomentosum* 'Shasta'.

V. plicatum var. formosanum Y C Liu & C H Ou   A shrub to 5 metres tall, with slender and densely stellate-tomentose branchlets. The leaves of pairs on flowering branches of unequal size. The fertile flowers very small, only about 3mm across.

V. plicatum f. *plicatum* f. *glabrum* **(Koidz ex Nakai) Rehd.**   The young branches are glabrescent with only scattered stellate hairs. The leaves are generally larger, 8-15cm long by 4-13cm wide, roundish or roundish-obovate to obovate, abruptly acuminate at the apex and with 9-15 pairs of lateral veins, glabrescent or minutely stellate-hairy beneath. The inflorescence is glabrescent or sparsely hairy. Intermediate forms are often found.

V. plicatum **var.** *parvifolium* **Miq.**   The young branches and inflorescence are stellate-pubescent. The leaves are smaller, 2-6cm long by 1-4cm wide, sparsely stellate-pubescent and later glabrate beneath with 8-12 pairs of lateral veins. Again intermediate forms are found and Hara treats this as only a geographical variety of the species.

Viburnum propinquum **Hemsl.** ❀ Journ. Linn. Soc. xxiii.355 (1888)

syn. *V. valerianicum* Elmer
Discovered by A Henry and introduced by Wilson in 1901.

A small bushy evergreen shrub with slender red-brown lustrous and strongly lenticellate branches from central and western China, Taiwan and the Philippines growing to 1 metre high by 1-1.5 metres across. The leaves ovate-lanceolate to oval, acute to long-acuminate at the apex, cuneate to broadly cuneate or rounded at the base, 3-veined, the outer pair arising somewhat above the base of the blade, arcuately ascending and anastomosing about half-way up the leaf blade, generally with a marginal gland on either side of the margin about 5 to 10mm above the petiole (sometimes two glands on one side), 5-8cm long by 2-3cm wide, the young shoots bronze at first turning shiny dark green above, lighter beneath, thinly coriaceous, glabrous on both sides except for some hairs in the vein-axils beneath. The petiole 6-12mm long, grooved above, glabrous. The flowers borne in June in terminal inflorescences 4-8cm across, the flowers greenish-white, 4mm across all, perfect. The fruit globose-ovoid, 5mm long by 4mm wide, blue-black.

V. propinquum 'Lanceolatum' ❀ A form with narrower leaves.

V. propinquum var. mairei W W Smith   The leaves which are linear-lanceolate and much smaller and narrower at 3-4.5cm long by 1-2cm wide, the apex is acute and not acuminate, the base narrowly cuneate. The inflorescence is smaller at 2-4cm across and the fruit 3-4mm long.

V. propinquum var. *parvifolium* **Graebn.** A small-leaved variety with finer textured foliage and a denser growth habit. The leaves are ovate and acuminate at the apex, do not exceed 4cm long and the fruit is about 3mm long.

Viburnum prunifolium **L.** ❀ Sp. Pl. 268 (1753)

syn. *V. pyrifolium* Poir. The black haw, or stag bush viburnum, often grown as a hedge as the branches have plenty of spur growth.

A large deciduous shrub or small tree from the eastern United States from Connecticut to Florida and west to Michigan and Texas growing to 4-6 metres high by 3-4 metres across. The leaves ovate, oval or obovate, blunt, rounded or slightly pointed at the apex, rounded or wedge-shaped at the base, finely serrate along the entire margin, 3-8cm long by 3-5cm wide, glabrous or nearly so, glossy dark green above, paler beneath, turning a rich wine-red in autumn. The petiole reddish, 8-20mm long, sometimes very narrowly winged. The flowers borne in June all perfect in short-stalked 3-4 rayed cymes 5-10cm across, the creamy-white to white flowers each 6mm in diameter, the anthers yellow-cream. The fruit oval to sub-globose, 10mm or more long, dark blue to black, bloomy, sweet and edible.

V. prunifolium var. *bushii* **(Ashe) Palmer & Steyerm.** The leaf shape is oblong-lanceolate and the petioles more winged. Occurring from southern Illinois to Arkansas.

V. prunifolium var. *globosum* **Nash.** The fruit are smaller at up to 6mm long and more globose in shape. Occurring in New Jersey and Pennsylvania.

V. prunifolium **'Gladwyne'** An exceptionally fine fruiting specimen growing in the garden of select native plants created by Mrs J Norman Henry of Gladwyne, Pennsylvania.

V. prunifolium **'Holden'** A weeping form selected by Lewis Lipp at the Holden Arboretum, Mentor, Ohio in about 1957 but subsequent correspondence suggests that this characteristic is not consistent.

V. prunifolium **'Mrs. Henry Large'** More compact with distinctly leathery green leaves in summer, turning maroon in autumn. The name apparently arose from a temporary label at Purdue University, Indiana, which referred to the origin of their cuttings (Miss or Mrs Henry) and the size of the original plant (large).

Viburnum rafinesquianum **Schult.** ❀ Syst. vi.630

syn. *V. affine* var. *hypomalacum* Blake, *V. pubescens* Rehd. not Pursch. The downy arrrowwood will grow happily in dry impoverished soil.

A hardy compact deciduous shrub from the eastern United States and Canada growing to 1.5-2 metres high, the same across. The leaves narrow to broad ovate, acute or acuminate at the apex, rounded or cordate at the base, coarsely toothed with 6-10 large triangular teeth on each side and 4-6 pairs of conspicuous and rather straight veins, 3-6cm long by 2-4cm wide, dull green and glabrous or nearly so above, densely pubescent beneath. The petiole very short, 2-6mm long, softly pubescent beneath with a pair of linear stipules at the base which are often longer than the petiole itself. The white flowers borne in May-June in abundant dense cymes up to 7cm across usually 5-7 rayed, each flower up to 6mm in diameter. The fruit ellipsoid, 8mm long, blue-black.

V. rafinesquianum var. *affine* (Bush) House The leaf stalks are longer at up to 20mm long and are usually longer than the stipules, the leaf is glabrous beneath except for some hairs on the veins towards the base and sometimes on the main veins throughout.

Viburnum recognitum Fern. ❀ Rhodora xliii.647 (1941)

Possibly syn. *V. dentatum* var. *lucidum* Ait.

A deciduous shrub from North America growing to 4-5 metres high by 3-4 metres across. The leaves of thin texture, ovate or broadly ovate, roundish, shortly acuminate at the apex, rounded or slightly cordate at the base, with 10-15 pairs of marginal teeth, usually large and triangular and with 6-8 vein pairs running from the midrib to the points of the teeth, some of these veins splitting before reaching the margin so that a vein terminates at the point of each tooth, 5-10cm long by 3-10cm wide, often broader than long, light green and glabrous above, light green beneath with a few hairs in the vein-axils. The petiole light green, 10-20mm long with a few hairs. The flowers borne in June-July white, perfect and regular about 4mm wide in corymbs up to 12cm wide on peduncles 3-6cm long. The fruit roundish oval, up to 10mm long, blue-black.

Viburnum x *rhytidocarpum* Lemoine ❀

A hybrid between *V. buddleifolium* and *V. rhytidophyllum*, useful as a semi-evergreen screen where rhododendrons will not grow.

A semi-evergreen shrub of hybrid origin growing to 3-4 metres high with a similar spread. The leaves ovate-oblong, acute at the apex, heart-shaped at the base, 15-20cm long by 4-6cm wide, entire or with a few crenate teeth, bright glossy green above, densely white pubescent beneath. The petiole 1-2cm long. The flowers borne in May-June are funnel-shaped 8mm across, all perfect in short-stalked, 7-rayed compound cymes 6-10cm across, light pink in bud opening white with prominent anthers. The fruit are oval, 8mm long, red turning black when ripe.

Viburnum x *rhytidophylloides* **Suringar** ❀ Jaarb. Nederl. Dendrol.
Vereen. (1927) p.140 and (1928) p.110

V. x rhytidophylloides originated from a *V. lantana* rootstock pollinated by *V. rhytidophyllum*; the original cross was made in Holland in about 1925 from which the original clone 'Holland', one of the first named hybrids, was named, although the cross occurs naturally in seed of *V. rhytidophyllum* when *V. lantana* is growing nearby.

A deciduous, or almost so, suckering shrub of cultivated hybrid origin growing to 4-5 metres high by 3-4 metres across. The leaves elliptic-ovate to ovate-oblong, pointed or blunt at the apex, rounded or slightly heart shaped at the base, 10-20cm long by 5-10cm wide, very dark, glossy green above, grey beneath. The petiole 1.5-3cm long. The flowers borne in May-June in large terminal umbel like trusses 10-20cm across, the flowers all fertile are a dull yellowish white, each about 6mm in diameter. The fruit oval, 8-10mm long, red at first, turning to a shining black, the clusters often containing both red and black fruit at the same time.

V. x rhytidophylloides **'Alleghany'** ❀ Introduced by the US National Arboretum in 1966, where a cross between *V. rhytidophyllum* and *V. lantana* 'Mohican' was self-pollinated to produce the F2 seedlings from which the cultivar was selected. 'Alleghany' is considered to have better foliage, flower and fruit than other selections with the same parentage. The fruits are very quickly taken by birds.

V. x rhytidophylloides **'Dart's Duke'** ❀ A selection from Darthuizer, Holland, growing to 3 metres with dull dark green broad-elliptic leaves 15-20cm long, persisting well into the winter. The yellowish-white flowers in wide-domed corymbs 14-18cm across, in May and June and often a second time in October-November.

V. x rhytidophylloides **'Holland'** The original hybrid with larger leaves than *V. rhytidophyllum*.

V. x rhytidophylloides **'Rhytana'** ❀ sometimes incorrectly named *V. x rhytana*. Originally introduced by R V Roger Ltd. of Pickering, Yorkshire, where it was discovered as a chance seedling in their nursery in early the 1990's. *V. lantana* pollinated by *V. rhytidophyllum* (as opposed to *V. x rhytidophylloides* where *V. rhytidophyllum* is the seed parent) it exhibits characteristics closer to *V. lantana*. The leaf is a lighter green and distinctly obovate, it is deciduous and the flower trusses are considerably smaller.

V. x rhytidophylloides **'Willowwood'** ❀ A cross made in 1928 by Henry Tubbs of Willowwood Farm, Gladstone, New Jersey. 'Willowwood' is said to be more resistant to wind damage and to have a longer flowering season, and purer white flowers than the type.

Viburnum rhytidophyllum **Hemsl.** ✿ Journ. Linn. Soc. xxiii.349 (1888)

Introduced by Wilson from central China for Messrs. James Veitch & Son in 1900. Hardy, though in hard winters the plant puts on a very dejected appearance, but best planted in a sheltered place, against a wall is ideal, as the large leaves can easily get wind-tattered. Not a plant for the small garden with its almost overpoweringly large and dark nature, *V. rhytidophyllum* is very striking when viewed from a distance in full flower and thrives in full sun. Indeed a distance away is the ideal place as the flowers, whilst magnificent in their intricacy, have a less than pleasant fragrance, described by Wilson as 'in large flat corymbs of dirty white flowers which are not very pleasing to the nostrils'. FCC 1907, AGM (1984).

A large evergreen shrub of suckering habit from central and western China growing to 6 metres high by 4 metres across. The leaves ovate-oblong, excessively wrinkled due to a dense network of deeply set veins, 10-20cm long by 3-6cm wide, very dark glossy green above, grey below with a starry down. the petiole 1.5-3cm long. The flowers borne in May are dull yellowish white about 5mm diameter borne in terminal 7-11-rayed trusses up to 20cm across; a full truss can contain more than 2500 individual flowers. The fruit oval, up to 1cm long, red turning shiny black.

V. rhytidophyllum '**Aldenham**' Pink flowers in broad clusters, the umbels of flowers larger than the type.

V. rhytidophyllum '**Roseum**' The flower buds are distinctly pink, thought only the slightest flush of this remains when the flowers open.

V. rhytidophyllum '**Variegatum**' ✿ syn. *V. rhytidophyllum* f. *aureovariegatum* Boom
A form with pale yellow and white variegation discovered before 1935 by Chenault in Orleans, France. Requires shade and older specimens may often revert if not carefully pruned.

Viburnum (rhytidophyllum **x** *utile)* '**Pragense**' ✿

syn. *V.* x *pragense* Hajek & Krouman
The original cross was made in 1955 at the Prague Municipal Gardens, Czech Republic. AGM 1993.

An evergreen shrub of cultivated hybrid origin growing to 3-5 metres high with the same spread. The leaves are elliptic or elliptic-lanceolate, 5-10cm long by 2.5-5cm wide, glossy green above, felty grey beneath. The petiole 15-30mm long. The pinkish-white flowers borne in May-June in large terminal umbel-like trusses 10-20cm across each flower 4-6mm across, the buds forming in autumn and remaining exposed during the winter. The fruit oval, 8mm long, red at first, turning shining black.

Viburnum rigidum **Vent.** ❀ Jard. Malm. 98

syn. *V. rugosum* Pers.
Introduced in 1778, only suitable for cultivation in temperate regions.

An erect evergreen shrub from the Canary Islands with branches bristly pubescent when young turning brown above, reddish beneath, growing to 3-4 metres high by 2-3 metres across. The leaves ovate to sub-orbicular, acute to acuminate at the apex, cuneate at the base, margins entire, 5-15cm long by 4-8cm wide, mid- to light green above, slightly lighter beneath, hairy on both sides, more so beneath when young, becoming smooth with age. The petiole 15-20mm long. The flowers borne in February-April pure white in wide cymes 7-10cm across, each flower 5-7mm across. The fruit ellipsoid, 6-7mm in diameter, dark brown turning to purple then blue-black.

Viburnum rufidulum **Raf.** ❀ Alsog. Am. 56

syn. *V. rufotomentosum* Small, *V. ferrugineum* Small, *V. prunifolium* var. *ferrugineum* Torrey & Gray.
The southern or rusty black haw is the southern equivalent of *V. prunifolium*. Introduced to Kew in 1902, it derives its common name from the velvety reddish down which covers the young shoots and the winter buds.

A large deciduous shrub or small tree of thin, rigid habit from the southern United States from Virginia to Florida growing to 10 metres high with a spread of 3-4 metres. The leaves elliptic, oval, ovate or obovate, rounded or slightly pointed at the apex, rounded or wedge-shaped at the base, finely serrate, 5-10cm long by 2-4cm wide, leathery, glossy dark green above, lighter beneath covered beneath with a short reddish down predominantly towards the base when young, turning maroon in winter. The petiole 6-12mm long, stout and usually narrowly winged and covered with reddish down. The flowers borne in May-June in cymes 8-12cm across, usually 4-rayed, the pure white flowers, all perfect, 8mm in diameter. The fruit ellipsoid, up to 15mm long, dark blue and bloomy.

V. rufidulum var. *floridanum* **Ashe.** Has more oblong leaves and scarcely glaucous fruits. Collected by Ashe in Walton County, Florida in 1923.

V. rufidulum var. *margarettae* **Ashe.** Has very broad, often sub-orbicular leaves, somewhat cordate at the base and the fruit are densely glaucous. Collected by Ashe at Groveton, E Texas, where it is the common form.

V. rufidulum **'Morton'** Introduced by the Morton Arboretum, Lisle, Illinois, and currently being evaluated (1999).

V. rufidulum **'Royal Guard'** ❀ A superior upright clone selected by Cole Nurseries, Circleville, Ohio.

Viburnum sargentii **Koehne** ❀ Gartenfl. 341 (1899)

Can be susceptible to spring frosts as the leaf growth starts early. AM 1967.

A deciduous suckering shrub from N-E Asia growing to 2-3 metres high with the same spread. The leaves 3 (sometimes 4 or 5)-lobed, maple-like, the base truncate, the lobes pointed, coarsely and irregularly toothed, the upper leaves generally have a more elongated middle lobe which is usually entire, occasionally the leaves are oblong-lanceolate without lobes, 8-12cm long, the same wide, young growth dark brown turning yellow green above, lighter beneath. The petiole 20-35mm long with large semi-circular glands at the base. The creamy-white flowers borne in May-June in cymes 8-10cm across, the outer, sterile flowers up to 3cm in diameter, the inner fertile flowers 4-5mm in diameter, the stamens with purple anthers. The fruit nearly globose, 10mm long, light red.

V. sargentii **'Onondaga'** ❀ Introduced by the US National Arboretum in 1966. The young foliage is a distinct deep bronze or maroon which it maintains even when mature before turning a chestnut-brown in autumn. The juvenile colouring can be enhanced by pruning to encourage new growth. The flower buds are the same deep maroon but the flowers open nearly white giving a splendid contrast against the dark foliage. The red fruits are effective against the dark foliage but are not abundantly produced. AGM 1993.

V. sargentii **f. *sterile* Hara.** A snowball form with all sterile flowers.

V. sargentii **'Susquehanna'** ❀ Introduced by the US National Arboretum in 1966, 'Susquehanna' was selected as a seedling from a batch of seed collected in Japan. It is noted for its heavily branched, corky trunk, upright growth habit, darker green leaves and abundance of flowers and fruit. The leaves can be as much as twice the size of those of the type, and the flower trusses up to 16cm across. The fruit are yellow-green in the summer, turning to a glossy dark red in autumn and persisting well into the winter.

Viburnum schensianum **Maxim.** Bull. Akad. Petersb. xxvi:480 (1880)

syn. *V. giraldii* Graebn. A thinly branched shrub with stellate-pubescent young branchlets, similar to *V. lantana*.

A deciduous shrub from N-W China growing to 3-4 metres with the same spread. The leaves are oval-elliptic, blunt or rounded at the apex, rounded or cuneate at the base, finely dentate with 5-6 vein-pairs usually dividing before reaching the margin, or partly ending in the teeth, 2-5cm long by 1.5-3cm wide, sparingly pubescent or glabrous above, stellate-pubescent beneath. The petiole 4-6mm long. The flowers borne in May-June in 5-rayed cymes 5-8cm across, each flower dullish white 6mm in diameter. The fruit ellipsoid, 8mm long, red turning black when ripe.

Viburnum setigerum **Hance** ❀ Journ.Bot. xx.261 (1882)

syn. *V. theiferum* Rehd.
Known as the tea viburnum as the leaves were used by the monks on Mount Omei to make a sweet tea said to have medicinal properties. Introduced by Wilson in 1901. Susceptible to late spring frosts. AM 1925.

A deciduous shrub from central and western China growing to 3-4 metres high by 2.5-3 metres across. The leaves ovate-lanceolate or oval-oblong, rounded at the base, widest beneath the middle and with a long, tapered point, sharply but remotely toothed, with 6-9 pairs of veins running out to the teeth, 8-15cm long by 3-6cm wide, dark green above, glabrous on both sides except for long silky hairs on the midrib and parallel veins beneath. The petiole 1-2.5cm long, glabrous or sparsely pubescent. The flowers borne in May-June white, all perfect 6mm wide in 5-rayed cymes 3-5cm across, terminal on short, lateral 2-leafed twigs. The fruit egg-shaped, 6-12mm long, red, becoming translucent after the first frosts.

V. setigerum 'Aurantiacum' ❀ Raised at the Arnold Arboretum from seed collected by Wilson in Chang-lo-hsien, Hupeh, China in 1907, selected for its fruit which changes from pale yellow to a strong orange as it ripens.

V. setigerum var. *sulcatum* Hsu The petiole is distinctly grooved.

Viburnum sieboldii Miq. ❀ Ann. Mus. Bot. Lugd. Bat. ii.267

Introduced from Japan by the Arnold Arboretum in 1880.

A large deciduous shrub or small tree from Japan, where it grows at altitudes of up to 900 metres on the slopes of Mount Fuji, with grey-brown branches and gnarled stems growing to 3-4 metres or more with the same spread. The leaves are elliptic to obovate or oblong, generally pointed, though sometimes rounded at the apex and cuneate or sometimes acute at the base, coarsely toothed along the edge of the top half of the leaf, 8-12cm long by 3-8cm wide and prominently veined with 7-10 pairs of parallel lateral nerves. They are dark glossy green above, lighter beneath, glabrous except for some hairs on the veins and in the vein-axils. The crushed leaves are aromatic, referred to variously as like green peppers, disagreeable or objectionable! The petiole is light green, 10-12mm long. The flowers borne in May-June are all perfect, creamy white in long-stalked cymes 8-10cm across on 2- or 4-leaved branchlets, each flower 8mm in diameter, with stamens shorter than the corolla-lobes. In climates with warmer summers and colder winters than the British Isles, the flowers often cover the entire plant and the fruit persist for more than three months before dropping but in the UK the maturing fruit which are oval, 12mm long and pink at first before turning blood red then blue-black, are often taken by birds before they are fully ripe, leaving the attractive red pedicels to provide a contrast against the dark green leaves.
According to Hara (1983) a rare variegated leaved form is cultivated in gardens in Japan.

V. sieboldii var. *longifolium* **Satake**   A form with oblanceolate leaves. However intermediate forms are common and Hara considers that this should not be recognized as a separate taxon.

V. sieboldii var. *reticulatum* **(Hort.) Rehd.** ❀ Smaller in every part; leaves glabrescent.

V. sieboldii var. *obovatifolium* **(Yanagita) Sugimoto** Leaves obovate or broadly so, often sharply serrate, to 25cm long. From the Japan Sea side of Honshu.

V. sieboldii **'Seneca'** ❀ Introduced by the US National Arboretum in 1966. Selected from a batch of self-pollinated seedlings for its greater abundance of flowers and fruit. Whilst the fruit of the type are generally taken by birds as soon as they are ripe, those of 'Seneca' do not suffer this fate, and persist well into the winter.

Viburnum suspensum **Lindl.** ❀ Journ. Hort. Soc. viii.130 (1853)

syn. *V. sandankwa* Hassk. *V. suspensum* appears to have been first introduced into the United Kingdom in about 1852 from the nursery of Mr van Houtte of Ghent, Belgium.

Very tender much branched evergreen shrub from south Japan, Taiwan and Indonesia growing to 1.5-3 metres high by 1.5-2 metres across. The leaves leathery, ovate or oval-elliptic, pointed or rounded at the apex, rounded or broadly wedge-shaped at the base, entire or shallowly dentate in the top half of the leaf blade with 4-5 vein-pairs 5-12cm long by 4-8cm wide, glossy dark green above, paler beneath, glabrous or with a few tufts of hairs in the vein-axils. The petiole 8-12mm long. The fragrant rose-tinted waxy white flowers borne in March to May in large terminal drooping panicles are often only conspicuous by their fragrance, 5-10cm wide, 2-4cm long, each flower 8mm in diameter, flowering on the previous year's branches. The fruit globose to ellipsoidal, about 5mm long, pale rose turning red then black.

Viburnum sympodiale **Graebner** ❀ Engl. Jahrb. xxix.587

Collected by Wilson in China in 1900. Closely allied to *V. lantanoides* and *V. furcatum*, from which it differs in having stipules on the leaf stalks and smaller, narrower, ovate and more finely toothed leaves which are sub-orbicular at the base.

A deciduous shrub from central China and Taiwan growing to 2-3 metres (up to 8 metres in the wild) by 2-2.5 metres across. The leaves are ovate to elliptic with a short, abrupt point at the apex and a heart-shaped base, irregularly and finely toothed, with 6-8 pairs of veins strongly ascending, indistinct on the upper surface and ending in the marginal teeth, the veinlets more or less parallel, distinct on the lower surface, 8-15cm long by 6-8cm wide, dark green above, downy when young turning glabrous, lighter and hairier beneath, especially on the veins and turning brilliant scarlet-red in autumn. The petiole 2-5cm long, densely stellate-pubescent and with stipules at the base. The flowers borne in May-June white in stalkless 5-rayed cymes 6-9cm across, the sterile outer flowers up to 20mm in diameter on long stalks, the central, fertile ones 4-5mm across. The fruit broadly oval, 8mm long, red at first, turning blackish-purple when ripe.

Viburnum taitoense **Hayata** Journ. Coll. Sc. Tokyo xxx.Art. 1.136 (1911)

Somewhat similar to *V. erubescens* but differing in the denser and shorter cymes, narrower leaves and calyx densely covered in stellate hairs. Distinguished from *V. suspensum* by the thinner and more pointed leaves which have more sharp teeth throughout the margin, the densely stellate pubescence and the calyx more hairy, especially in the upper part.

A small evergreen shrub from Taiwan growing to 1.5-2 metres high with a similar spread. The leaves oblong-lanceolate, acute to obtuse at the apex, acute at the base, sharply roundish-mucronate toothed with 5-6 pairs of arcuate lateral veins, the midrib and veins impressed above, raised beneath, 5-8cm long by 2-3cm wide, thinly coriaceous, glabrous on both sides, dark and shiny above, paler beneath, the petiole 5-10mm long, sulcate, pubescent. The white flowers in short terminal rounded pubescent cymes 3cm across, the flowers are all fertile, each flower about 5mm in diameter. The fruit ovoid, slightly pubescent, 8mm long, red.

Viburnum taiwanianum **Hayata** ✿ Journ. Coll. Sc. Tokyo xxx. Art 1.137 (1911)

Similar to *V. urceolatum* but the leaves tend to be almost entire or only obscurely toothed, and are more acuminate; there are also differences in the veination. However Hara (1983) notes that plants of *V. urceolatum* with elongated leaves have been found in Japan and variability in the flowers leads him to suggest a unification of the two species.

A straggly deciduous shrub from central and southern Taiwan growing to 2 metres high with a similar spread. The leaves ovate-oblong to oblong-lanceolate, broadly acuminate at the apex, obtuse to rounded at the base, finely toothed or almost entire with 4-5 pairs of lateral veins, 8-15cm long by 4-6cm wide, glabrous dark green above, paler beneath with stellate-pubescence on the veins. The petiole 20mm long, stellate-pubescent. The white flowers borne on the current year's growth in terminal compound cymes, 4-6cm across, each 2-3mm across. The fruit ellipsoid, 6mm long by 4mm across, red at first, turning black.

Viburnum tinus **L.** ✿ Sp. Pl. 267 (1753)

Commonly known as laurustinus from its shiny evergreen laurel-like leaves. It has a dense habit and keeps its leaves right down to the ground which makes it a very useful when planted as a hedge. In any event, its winter flowering, even if the fragrance does not match that of *V. x bodnantense* or *V. farreri*, make it a worthwhile addition to any garden. Said to have been introduced to Britain at the end of the 16th Century. AGM (1969)

An evergreen shrub from S Europe and N Africa growing to 3-4 metres high by 3-5 metres across. The leaves narrowly ovate or oblong and entire, acute at both ends, 3-10cm long by 2-4cm wide, dark green and glossy above, lighter beneath with tufts of down in the lower vein-axils. The petiole 1.5-2cm long, sometimes slightly hairy. The flowers borne from November-April are slightly fragrant, white or pinkish-white, all uniform and perfect in flattish or slightly convex, terminal cymes 5-8cm across, each flower about 6mm in diameter. The fruit ovoid, tapering towards the top, 6mm long, dark blue turning black.

V. tinus **'Aureo-Marginatum'** A form with the margin edged in yellow which received an Award in the 1880's but is probably now lost.

V. tinus **'Bewley's Variegated'** ❀ A variegated form growing to 3 metres high, indistinguishable from *V. tinus* 'Variegatum'.

V. tinus **'Eve Price'** ❀ With smaller leaves, selected for its compact habit and carmine buds opening to white tinged with pink. AM 1961, AGM (1984)1993.

V. tinus **'Exbury'** ❀ The flower trusses and the flowers themselves are larger, the trusses measuring up to 12cm across, whilst each flower is up to 12mm in diameter with very prominent anthers. The cultivar has an excellent fragrance but does not flower until April-May. Stems and leaf stalks green except for a touch of red at the base of the leaf stalk.

V. tinus **'French White'** ❀ A stronger-growing form distinguished by the hairiness of the young stems, the leaves which are not as glossy, and the flowers are larger and more purely white. Commonly sold for hedging.

V. tinus **'Froebelii'** Originally documented in the *Kew Handlist of Trees and Shrubs* in 1894, said to have a compact habit and white flowers, but almost certainly lost to cultivation.

V. tinus **'Gwenllian'** ❀ Discovered by Sydney Pearce, Assistant Curator of Kew from 1946 - 1970, and selected for its flower trusses which are smaller but more numerous, the flowers remaining tinged with pink; it is named after his wife. Certificate of Preliminary Commendation 1975, AGM (1984)1993.

V. tinus **f. *hirtum* Ait.** ❀ Larger but less hardy than the type. Leaves 8-10cm long, 4-5cm wide, rounded or heart-shaped at the base. The shoots, flower and leaf stalks and the bases of the leaves are covered with bristly hairs. AM 1939.

V. tinus 'Israel' ❀ The flower are borne in larger, flatter trusses which open 4 to 6 weeks later than the type.

V. tinus **'Little Bognor'** ❀ A compact free flowering selection.

V. tinus **'Lucidum'** ❀ A strong-growing cultivar with glabrous, burnished young shoots and glossy leaves. The leaves and flower trusses are larger, and the flowers can be up to 12mm in diameter in corymbose panicles up to 8cm across. It is not hardy and tends to flower later and for a shorter period. AM 1972.

V. tinus **'Lucidum Variegatum'** ❀ As *V. tinus* 'Lucidum' but with yellow variegation to the leaves.

V. tinus **'Macrophyllum'** ❀ The leaves are larger, up to 15cm long and 8cm wide.

V. tinus **'Pink Prelude'** ❀ A compact growing form with distinctly pink flowers opening white later in the season.

V. tinus **'Port of Nice'** A chance seedling growing beside the War Memorial overlooking the Port of Nice selected by Treseder's Nurseries, Cornwall in 1962, the flowers are blush pink and the leaves broader than the type at up to 9 by 4.5cm.

V. tinus **'Purpureum'** ❀ The leaves are darker green and tinged with purple when young.

V. tinus **'Pyramidale'** ❀ syn. *V. tinus* 'Strictum'. A more narrow and upright cultivar thought to be freer flowering and fruiting.

V. tinus **'Robustum'** A strongly upright cultivar, said to be resistant to mildew. Not now known in cultivation.

V. tinus **'Roseum'** A pink budded sport, probably lost to cultivation.

V. tinus **'Spring Beauty'** Discovered in a private garden in Cornwall in 1967 by Neil Treseder of Treseder's Nurseries. A compact bush with small, pointed leaves 6cm by 2.5 cm, the flowers are pure white.

V. tinus **'Spring Bouquet'** Introduced in America in about 1955/7. A dwarf bush growing to about 1.5 metres, the buds red, opening to white and almost covering the plant in early spring.

V. tinus **'Variegatum'** ❀ Noticeably less hardy and with distinctly variegated leaves where whole portions, sometimes half the blade, are creamy-yellow.

Viburnum trilobum **Marsh.** ❀ Arbust. Am. 162

syn.*V. opulus* 'Americanum' Ait., *V. americanum* Rehd., *V. oxycoccus* Pursh., *V. opuloides* Muhl.

The American cranberrybush. Hardier than *V. opulus* growing far north into Canada, and best in moist acid conditions. The fruit are edible and more palatable than those of *V. opulus*; in America they are used to make jam or jelly. Very similar to *V. opulus* from which it is distinguished by the petiole which has small glands at the base and is only shallowly grooved and the central lobe of the leaf is more elongated.

A deciduous suckering shrub from the northern states of North America and Canada growing to 2-3 metres high with the same spread. The leaves broad ovate, three-lobed, the lobe tips acuminate, rounded or truncate at the base, the lobes generally coarsely dentate although sometimes the central lobe is elongated and entire, 5-12cm long, the same wide, glabrous light green above, lighter and slightly pubescent beneath, turning deep red in autumn. The petiole 1-3cm long with a shallow groove and small, usually stalked columnar glands which are round-topped and as long as or longer than they are thick, also with thick-tipped and bluntish stipules. The flowers borne in May-June have an outer ring of large sterile flowers each up to 2cm in diameter surrounding a centre of small fertile flowers which are much smaller at 6-8mm in diameter, all white in cymes 7-10cm across. The fruit nearly globose, 9mm long, scarlet-red.

In the early twentieth century A E Morgan undertook a study of *V. trilobum* at East Lee, Massachusetts with a view to improving the species. Seed from many of the northern states of North America and Canada, from Alaska to Newfoundland were observed and selected, the plants being assembled in a plantation of some 3,300 plants in the Berkshire Mountains, Massachusetts, in 1915. In 1921 the study was taken over by the US Department of Agriculture, and in 1922 three of the best selections were named; 'Andrews', 'Hahs' and 'Wentworth' and were released to the trade. Unfortunately the plantation was abandoned after 10 years and by 1960 had been all but obliterated to make way for the Massachusetts Turnpike.

V. trilobum **'Alfredo'** has a denser, broader habit with excellent autumn colour but poor fruit-set. Selected by Bailey Nursery, USA, and named after a long time employee of theirs, Alfredo 'Freddie' Garcia.

V. trilobum **'Andrews'** (Selected in 1917 by Frank Andrews, one of the field collectors for A E Morgan.) 'Andrews' is a sturdy, erect grower with dark green foliage and smaller than the type, growing to only 2 metres. The fruit ripen later and are larger than those of other cultivars, they are held erect by stout stems and have the highest pectin content of any variety.

V. trilobum **'Compactum'** ❀ syn. *V. trilobum* 'Bailey Compact'. A small bush growing to 1.5 metres with dense growth on many thin stems but fruiting less heavily.

V. trilobum **'Garry Pink'** Discovered by Professor Walker at the Wildwood Golf Club, Fort Garry, Manitoba in 1962. The flowers are noticeably pink only when the weather is cool and moist at flowering time, in hot, dry conditions the flowers are white.

V. trilobum **'Hahs'** ❀ Selected in 1915 by Roy(Ray?) Hahs, one of A E Morgan's field collectors. 'Hahs' was selected for its vigorous growth, its abundance of fruit and its high pectin content. Frequently mis-named as 'Hans'.

V. trilobum **'Manito'** Named by Dr R Leslie of the Morden Experimental Farm, Morden, Manitoba in 1947. 'Manito' was discovered growing in the wild by an Indian at the south end of Lake Manitoba and was selected for the size of its fruit.

V. trilobum **'Phillips'** was selected by Elwyn Meader and introduced in 1956 by the University of New Hampshire, Durham, from a plant found by a Mr. Phillips on a roadside in Acton, Maine. It is free of the odour and flavour typical of the type and flowers and fruits abundantly, the fruits which are a deep wine-red, being used for making jelly.

V. trilobum **'Redwing'** The young leaves and petioles are reddish and remain more or less so throughout the season.

V. trilobum **'Spring Green Compact'** growing to little more than 1 metre with excellent red fruit and orange-red autumn colour.

V. trilobum **'Spring Red Compact'** similar to 'Spring Green Compact' but the young growth is red, turning green with age.

V. trilobum **'Wentworth'** ❀ was also selected by Frank Andrews, being named after the farm of O E Wentworth near Lancaster, New Hampshire where the original clone was discovered. 'Wentworth' has a more spreading habit and the fruit, which are slightly larger, mature earlier in drooping clusters.

Viburnum urceolatum **Sieb. & Zucc.** Abh. Akad. Muench. iv.III 172 (1846)

A straggling deciduous shrub from Japan, China and Taiwan growing up to 1 metre high by 2-3 metres or more by self-layering. The leaves ovate to lanceolate, acuminate to acute at the apex, obtuse to rounded or cordate at the base, obtusely serrulate or sub-entire, with 4-5 pairs of lateral veins impressed on the upper surface, raised beneath, 6-12cm long by 2-2.5cm wide, deep green and glabrous above, pale green and minutely stellate-pubescent beneath, especially on the veins. The petiole 1-2cm long, stellate pubescent. The white flowers borne in May-June white, in 5-rayed cymes 3-6cm across, each flower 2-3mm across. The fruit ovate to ellipsoid, 6mm long by 4mm across, red turning black.

V. urceolatum f. *procumbens* **(Nakai) Hara** A low shrub often less than 50cm high with long creeping stems which root readily, found in the damp coniferous woods in the central and northern districts of Honshu.

Viburnum utile Hemsl. ❀ Journ. Linn. Soc. xxiii.356 (1888)

Originally discovered by Mr Thomas Watters of the British Consular service in 1879-80 near Ichang, but not introduced into Britain until 1901 when Wilson sent a specimen to Messrs James Veitch & Sons. AM 1926.

A graceful evergreen shrub of open habit from China growing to 1-2 metres high with a spread of 2 metres or more. The leaves narrowly ovate or nearly oblong, tapered but blunted at the apex, rounded or wedge-shaped at the base, with 5-6 vein-pairs very prominent beneath, margins entire, 3-7cm long by 1-3cm wide, dark glossy green above, almost white beneath with a thick, starry down. The petiole 6-12mm long. The flowers borne in May all fertile white in dense 5-rayed rounded terminal cymes, 5-8cm across, each waxy flower 10mm wide. The fruit oval, 6mm long, blue-black.

V. utile **var.** *elaeagnifolium* **Rehd.** Differs from the type in its slender branchlets, yellowish tomentum, leaves which are thinner and oblong-lanceolate, more slender petiole, yellowish-green above, corymbs smaller and with fewer flowers, about 3cm in diameter.

Viburnum veitchii C. H. Wright ❀ Gard. Chron. I.257 (1903)

Similar to *V. lantana* but more ornamental. Introduced by Wilson in 1901.

A deciduous shrub from China growing to 1-2 metres high by 1 metre across. The leaves ovate, pointed at the apex, heart-shaped to rounded at the base, sharply and widely dentate, 7-12cm long by 5-8cm wide, the underside grey-green densely covered with stellate hairs. The petiole short, up to 10mm long. The flowers borne in May-June in short-stalked flat cymes 8-12cm across, usually 7-rayed, white uniform and perfect 6mm in diameter. The fruit short ellipsoid, 8mm long, red at first, turning black when ripe.

Viburnum wilsonii Rehd. Sargent, Trees and Shrubs ii.115 (1908)

Discovered by Wilson in 1904 and introduced by him in 1908 from Sichuan. The young shoots very downy becoming dark purplish with age. Similar to *V. mullaha* which is distinguished by the fasciculate-pilose indumentum to the inflorescence, and the pubescence on the underside of the leaf.

A deciduous shrub from central and W China growing to 2-3 metres with the same spread. The leaves are ovate to roundish oval, long slender pointed at the apex, rounded or broadly tapering at the base, toothed along the whole of the edge, with 6-7 vein-pairs running out to the teeth, 4-8cm long by 2-4cm wide, the young growth bronze-brown becoming dark green and with a few simple or forked hairs above, paler and glabrous beneath except for some long hairs on the veins. The petiole 10-15mm long, hairy without stipules. The flowers pinkish-white, all fertile borne in June in 6-rayed terminal corymbs 5-6cm across, each flower 6mm in diameter, the peduncle about 2cm long with a yellowish velvety pubescence. The fruit ovate, 8mm long, bright red and downy.

Viburnum wrightii **Miq.** ❦ Ann. Mus. Bot. Lugd. Bat. ii.267

Originally collected by Sargent in Japan in 1892, *V. wrightii* is closely related to *V. dilatatum* from which it is distinguished by all the parts of the plant which are are less downy and the fruits which are larger.

An upright deciduous shrub with dark brown bark from Japan and Korea growing to 2-3 metres high by 1.5-2.5 metres across. The leaves obovate to nearly circular on flowering shoots, more ovate or broadly ovate on longer non-flowering shoots, abruptly acuminate at the apex, rounded or broadly heart-shaped, sometimes tapered, at the base, coarsely dentate with 6-10 pairs of veins, 8-14cm long by 5-8cm wide, bright green and glabrous above, lighter beneath with tufts of hairs in the vein-axils, with 1-4 small dark circular glands on the underside close to the base, turning brown-red in autumn. The petiole 6-15mm long, purplish-red, estipulate, rarely stipulate. The flowers borne in May-June white, all fertile in 5-rayed cymes 5-10cm across, each flower 5-7mm in diameter. The fruit round-ovoid or globose, 8 -10mm long, glossy scarlet in August, persisting for several months.

V. wrightii var. *eglandosum* **Nakai** ❦ Lacks the dark circular glands on the underside near the base of the leaf.

V. wrightii '**Hessei**' ❦ syn *V. hessii* Koehne, *V. wrightii* var. *hessii* (Koehne) Rehd. First described in 1909 as a new species introduced by Herman Hesse grown from seed collected by Sergeant in Japan and put into commerce the following winter. More compact growing to less than 2 metres high. Leaves more ovate up to 11cm long, flatter and more sparsely dentate turning brilliant red in autumn. Smaller flower cymes only up to 6cm across, fruiting freely.

GLOSSARY

This is a brief Glossary intended to cover some of the more unusual botanical terms that have been used in the text. For a more comprehensive coverage see HARRIS, J G & HARRIS, M W in the Bibliography.

actinomorphic - (flowers) possessing radial symmetry
acuminate - gradually tapering to a sharp point
acute - tapering to a point at the apex with an angle less than 90°
adnate - attached by its whole length
albumen - the part of the seed from which a plant grows
anastomosing - (leaf veins) branching and rejoining to form a network
anther - the pollen-bearing part of the stamen
arcuate - curved in an arc
bract - a leaf-like structure beneath the flower or pedicel
caducous - falling early (sometimes referred to as 'early deciduous')
calyx - the leaf-like outer parts of the flower
campanulate - bell-shaped
chartaceous - (of leaves) with a papery texture
cordate - heart-shaped
coriaceous - (of leaves) with a leathery texture
corolla - the flower tube and petals
corymb - a more or less flat-topped inflorescence
crenate - rounded (teeth on a leaf margin)
cuneate - wedge-shaped, tapering to a point at the base
cyme - a more rounded inflorescence than a corymb
cymose - arranged in cymes
dehiscent - (seed) splitting open to release seed when ripe
dentate - toothed along the margin with the teeth pointing outwards
denticulate - as dentate but with smaller teeth
discoid - shaped like a disc
dorsifix - attached by its dorsal surface
drupe - a fruit with a fleshy outside covering a hard stone with a single seed
ellipsoid - shaped like an ellipse
elliptic - a narrow oval, broadest at the middle with the ends more or less equal
endocarp - the hard outer shell containing the seed
entire - the margin of the leaf without any teeth
estipulate - without stipules
evanescent - remaining only for a short time
fasciculate - arranged in bundles (of hairs on a leaf surface)
ferrugineous - coloured rusty red
filament - the stalk bearing the anther
fulvous - coloured dull yellowish-brown

glabrous - smooth, without hairs
glabrate - almost glabrous
globose - more or less spherical
hermaphrodite - having both male and female parts in the same flower
hypocrateriform - shaped like a platter
indumentum - dense hairy covering of a leaf
inflorescence - the flower cluster
lanceolate - lance-shaped with the widest point below the middle
membranaceous - thin, soft and flexible
mucro - a short sharp point at the apex or on the margin of the leaf
oblanceolate - as lanceolate but with the widest point above the middle
oblate - a sphere flattened at the poles
oblong - similar to elliptic but with the central part more or less parallel
obovate - as ovate but with the broadest part above the centre
obtuse - blunt or rounded at the apex with an angle greater than 90°
orbicular - almost circular
oval - as elliptic but broader
ovate - egg-shaped with the broadest part below the centre
ovoid - egg-shaped
ovule - the part of the ovary developing into the seed when fertilized
palmate - with three or more lobes
panicle - a rounded or pyramidal inflorescence
pedicel - the stalk of a single flower
peduncle - the stalk of the whole inflorescence
petiolate - having a petiole
petiole - the leaf stalk
pilose - with long, soft mainly straight hairs
pistil - the whole female reproductive organs of a flower
pinnate - with three or more leaflets in opposite rows
polymorphic - having variable forms - within a species
pubescent - covered with hairs, generally short
pyrene - the seed and its outer covering (endocarp)
retuse - with a shallow notch at the apex
rhombic - shaped as the diamond in a pack of playing cards
ruminate - soft and mobile as if chewed
serrate - saw-toothed along the margin with the teeth pointing upwards
sessile - attached directly without a stalk
spheroid - almost spherical, but elliptic in cross-section
stamen - the male part of the flower comprising the anther and the filament
stellate - star-shaped (hairs with several radiating from a base)
stigma - the end of the pistil which receives the pollen
stipule - a narrow leaf-like appendage at the base of the stipule (often in pairs)
stipulate - having stipules
style - the part of the pistil between the stigma and the ovary

sub- (prefix) - meaning almost, somewhat
tomentose - with a covering of short hairs
tomentum - a covering of short hairs
trifid - split into three lobe-like divisions
truncate - more or less squared at the base or apex
umbel - a flat-topped inflorescence
vein-axil - the area formed by the acute angle between two veins
zygomorphic - symmetrical along a single axis

BIBLIOGRAPHY

BARTRUM, D	*Hydrangeas and Viburnums.* (1958)
BEAN, W J (Ed.)	*Trees and Shrubs Hardy in the British Isles.* 8th. Ed. revised (1980).
BURKWOOD & SKIPWITH Ltd	*Catalogue of Flowering Shrubs* (1929)
DIRR, M	*Manual of Woody Landscape Plants.* 5th Ed. (1998)
EGOLF, D R	Am. Hort. Mag. 41 pp.139-155 *Ornamental deciduous flowering Viburnums* (1962)
EGOLF, D R	Am. Hort. Mag. 41 pp.209-224 *Ornamental fruiting and autumnal foliage Viburnums.* (1962)
EGOLF, D R	Am. Hort. Mag. 42 pp. 39-51 - *Evergreen Viburnums.* (1963)
EGOLF, D R	American Nurseryman pp. 46-56 *National Arboretum releases ten new Viburnums.* (1967)
EGOLF, D R	Am. Nurseryman. *The National Arboretum introduces 'Apache', 'Chippewa' and 'Huron'.* (July 1987)
EGOLF, D R	Am. Nurseryman. *Eight new ornamentals from the US National Arboretum.* (Apr. 1987)
EGOLF, D R	Am. Nurseryman. *Rising Stars* (Conoy Viburnum). (Jan. 1989)
EGOLF, D R	Baileya 14:24-28 *Two new cultivars of Viburnum, 'Cayuga' and 'Mohawk'.* (1966)
EGOLF, D R	ibid. 14:106-122 *Eight new viburnum cultivars.* (1966)
EGOLF, D R	ibid. 18:23-5 *Viburnum dilatatum 'Erie'.* (1971)
EGOLF, D R	U S National Arboretum (14 p. Index). *The Cultivated Viburnums.* (1962)
EGOLF, D R	Hort. Science 14:78-79 *'Shasta' Viburnum.* (1979)
EGOLF, D R	ibid. 16:350 *'Chesapeake' Viburnum.* (1981)
EGOLF, D R	ibid. 16:691 *'Eskimo' Viburnum.* (1981)
EGOLF, D R	ibid. 21:1077-8 *'Shoshoni' Viburnum.* (1986)
EGOLF, D R	ibid. 22:174-176 *'Chippewa' and 'Huron' Viburnum.* (1987)
EGOLF, D R	ibid. 23:419-421 *'Conoy' Viburnum.* (1988)
EGOLF, D R	Journ. Arn. Arb. 43 pp.132-172. *A cytological study of the Genus Viburnum.* (1962)
EGOLF, D R	Plantations Vol. XVIII. *Viburnums for the North.* (Spring 1962)
FARRER, R	*On the Eaves of the World* Vol I pp.96-7 (1917)
GLEASON (Ed.)	*New Britton and Brown Illustrated Flora of the North Eastern USA and Canada.* Vol 3. (1958)
HARA, H	Ginkgoana No. 5 *A Revision of the Caprifoliaceae of Japan.* (1983)

HARRIS, J G & M W
Plant Identification Terminology - An Illustrated
Glossary (1997).

HOOKER, W J
Flora boreali-Americana. vol.I pp.279-281 (1833)

HOOKER, J D (C B CLARKE)
Flora of British India. Vol. iii. (1880)

HOUTMAN, R T
Dendroflora Nr. 35 pp. 96-148. Viburnum. (1998)
Journal of the Royal Horticultural Society. (ab
initio.)

KANEHIRA
Formosan Trees (1936)

KERN, J H
Reinwardtia vol.1 pt.2:107-170. The Genus
Viburnum in Malaysia. (1951)

KILLIP & SMITH
Bull. Torr. Bot. Cl. lvi:265-274. The Genus
Viburnum in northwestern South America. (1929)

KRUSSMANN, G
Manual of Cultivated Broad-leaved Trees and
Shrubs. (1978).

LANCASTER, R
The Garden 125:11 pp. 822-3 Viburnum
Conundrum (2000)

LI, H L
Woody Flora of Taiwan. (1963)

LUNDELL
Lloydia. Vol. 2, Pt. 2. Mexican and Central
American Plants. (1939)

LUNDELL
Wrightia. Vol. 3 Pt. 8. American Plants. (1966)

MALECOT, V
Approche Systématique et Phylogénétique du
genre Viburnum. (Unpub. 1997)

McATEE, W L
A review of the Neartic Viburnum (1956)

MORTON, C V
Contributions from the U.S.National
Herbarium.Vol. 26(7). The Mexican & Central
American Species of Viburnum. (1933)

MORTON, C V
Proc. Biol. Soc. of Washington. Vol. 49. pp
153-154 Some Guatemalan species of Viburnum.
(1936)

OHWI, J
Flora of Japan. (1965)
The Plant Finder. (ab initio)

REHDER, A
Bibliography of cultivated Trees and Shrubs. (1949)

REHDER, A
Manual of cultivated Trees and Shrubs. (1940)

REHDER, A
Sargent Trees and Shrubs. Vol II (1908)

RIDLEY
Flora of the Malay Peninsular. Vol II. (1923)

THOMAS, G S
Ornamental Shrubs, Climbers and Bamboos. (1992)

TORREY, J & GRAY, A
A Flora of North America. (1838/43, reprinted
1969)

U S NATIONAL ARBORETUM
Viburnum Cultivar Checklist - Rough Notes
(Unpub. 1993)

WYMAN, D
Arnoldia pp. 47-56. Viburnums. (1959)

AVAILABILITY

Viburnums are widely available, indeed it would be hard to find a shrub nursery which did not have a reasonable slection, and *The RHS Plant Finder* lists a very comprehensive selection for the UK buyer. Below is a slection of nurseries from which many of the plants in the Collection have been obtained.

Bridgemere Nurseries, Nantwich, Cheshire.
Crug Farm Gardens, Caernarfon, Gwynedd.
Dingle Nurseries, Welshpool, Powys.
Pieter Zwijnenburg, Boskoop, Holland.
Pleasant View Nursery, Newton Abbot, Devon.
PMA Plant Specialities, Taunton, Somerset.
The Place for Plants, East Bergholt, Suffolk.

There are two other viburnum National Plant Collections® in the UK:

Derby City Council, Darley Abbey Park, Derby.
The RHS Garden, Hyde Hall, Essex.

In Europe a number of countries have similar schemes to the National Plant Collections®, many plants and much cutting material has come from:

Pepinieriste Maurice Laurent, St Romain en Gal, Lyon, France
Ward van Teylingen, Boskoop, Netherlands